THE AFTERLIFE REVOLUTION

WHITLEY AND ANNE STRIEBER

WALKER & COLLIER, INC., PUBLISHERS

The Afterlife Revolution

by Whitley and Anne Strieber

Walker & Collier, Inc, Publishers

Walker & Collier, Inc. 20742 Stone Oak Parkway Suite 107

San Antonio, Texas, 78258

www.unknowncountry.com

First Walker & Collier printing, first edition, 2017

Library of Congress Cataloging-in-Publication Data

Strieber, Whitley, Strieber, Anne

The afterlife revolution / by Whitley and Anne Strieber

ISBN (Paperback) 978-0-9742865-7-0

(Electronic Book) 978-0-9742865-6-3

(Audio Book) 978-0-9742865-8-7

❀ Created with Vellum

Mankind is a species divided, not so much between the sexes but between the living and what are called the dead. It isn't natural and it isn't necessary. We can become whole.

--Anne Strieber

ACKNOWLEDGMENTS

We would like to thank Belle Fuller, William and Clare Henry, Trish and Rob MacGregor, Leigh McCloskey and Alex Rotaru for allowing us use their names in our reporting of what they witnessed, and Dr. Patricia Turrisi for her invaluable advice and insights, and all of our other early readers who were kind enough to explore our journey with us during the writing of this book, and most especially Dr. Gary Schwartz for his foreword.

--Anne and Whitley Strieber

FOREWORD

Gary E. Schwartz, PhD

"All through history, there have been those who have lived in conscious relationship with Earth and the cosmos. We call them masters. In the future, everybody who enters the physical will do so as a master of being. And why will we still be using the physical? Give somebody a kiss. That's why. Humanity's destiny in the universe is to bring forth the experience of love, that all may share in it. Objective love, the core creative urgency, is also the essential human energy....Enlightenment is what happens when there is nothing left of us but love."

--Anne Strieber

"Incredibly, Anne has managed to provide what for me on a personal level must be final proof. She has done something that once goes to the heart of our relationship and also explores the deepest meaning of death, dying, and living on. I will devote the final chapter of this book to it, but know that, from the time it happened just a few days ago, my position has changed. I now feel certain that Anne still exists, and with her I must also assume the legions of the dead, all still very real, but in ways that we have scarcely even begun to understand."

--Whitley Strieber

Is life after death real? Is there a greater reality beyond our five senses? Can we personally know, for sure, whether our loved ones' consciousness continues after physical death? And can we grow into this emerging knowledge and wisdom as individuals and a species?

According to Anne and Whitley Strieber, the inspired authors of The Afterlife Revolution, the answers to these profound questions are emphatically yes.

I have read many books on near death experiences, after death communications, observations made by gifted evidential mediums, and afterlife science. I have written forewords for some of these books, and I have also written a few spiritual science books myself, including The Afterlife Experiments and The G.O.D. Experiments.

However, the Afterlife Revolution stands out among these books in terms of its scope, beauty, and lessons for all of us. Despite the well-known controversies surrounding the authors of this extraordinary book – for example, their reported observations of aliens – and maybe because of their historic openness to the existence of intelligent life beyond planet Earth, their personal journey following Anne's physical death takes on additional importance and meaning.

One of the reasons I felt compelled to write a foreword for this book was to honor the inspiring nature of the breadth and depth of Anne and Whitley's love for each other, both before and after Anne's physical death, coupled with the intense intellectual curiosity they shared for understanding life and the cosmos. We will return to the importance of love, especially objective love, at the end of this foreword.

However, another reason I had to write this foreword was because of the surprising and compelling spontaneous evidence that emerged for the presence of Anne in my professional and personal world following the beginning of my reading of this book!

Let's consider this extraordinary evidence for Anne's presence first, and then return to the Afterlife Revolution. I have provided enough details below so that you can appreciate, and appropriately evaluate, the convincing nature of this evidence.

On Thursday morning, September 14, 2017, Rhonda (my wife) and I were preparing to drive to Scottsdale, Arizona, where I would be giving two presentations at the Afterlife Research and Education Institute Conference (www. afterlifestudies.org). The lecture on Friday afternoon was titled "Lessons from mediumship science for spirit communication technology research." The other was a Saturday night banquet presentation titled "How science is proving that spirits are collaborating with us."

The evening banquet was coincidently hosted by George Noory of Coast to Coast AM. Whitley had co-authored a bestselling book with Art Bell, the prior award winning host of Coast to Coast AM. Their book, The Coming Global Superstorm, inspired the popular movie The Day After Tomorrow.

I had just started reading The Afterlife Revolution, and the thought popped into my head that maybe I could obtain some independent evidence of Anne's continued consciousness.

In an early morning meeting with Rhonda and a team of "hypothesized collaborating spirits," Rhonda – a selective research medium who describes her journey to this unusual profession in her book Love Eternal – asked Susy Smith, an active member of the spirit team, if she could locate Anne and bring her to two different evidential mediums who would be presenting at the Scottsdale conference. We call this the "double-deceased" paradigm, where one deceased person (e.g. Susy) brings another deceased person (e.g. Anne) to a medium under blinded conditions. Rhonda's sense was that Susy was present at our meeting and that Susy would try to do so. Susy has successfully employed the double-deceased paradigm with these two mediums on multiple occasions. FYI, unlike Rhonda and Whitley, I do not have mediumistic or channeling skills, and I do not see or hear spirit. In fact, one of my former research colleagues, Dr. Robert Stek, refers to me as the "Helen Keller of afterlife research."

Anyway, after our meeting, I was inspired to text two research mediums and alert them to the possibility that Susy might be attempting to contact them with a mystery deceased person. To help them connect with the second deceased person, I provided Anne's first name. Since neither medium knew that I was currently reading Whitley's unpublished book, it is probable that they would have no idea that Anne X was actually Anne Strieber. At this point Rhonda did not know that I had texted the two mediums.

Meanwhile, unbeknownst to me, Rhonda had reconnected with the Team and suggested that they could either (1) attempt to connect with the mediums and bring through evidence relative to our current research, or (2) be creative and bring through any other potentially relevant evidence. What Rhonda heard next was utterly novel which she later shared with me.

The phrase that she clearly heard in what she calls her "mind's ear" was "Listen to the wind whistling through the pines." She was not sure who said this atypical, poetic-type phrase. And she had no idea what, if anything, this might be referring to.

When Rhonda told me this, I wondered if it was possible whether Susy (and Anne?) might have been aware of my decision to text the two mediums, and I pondered whether the "listen to the wind whistling through the pines" phrase might somehow relate to Whitley and/or Anne.

I immediately emailed Whitley. I mentioned the context and the phrase and explained that we needed to keep him blind to the identity of the spirit who might have shared the utterance. I had no idea if this phrase would have (1) no significance, (2) a vague, general meaning, if not (3) a highly specific one. What Whitley wrote back was completely unexpected.

In the draft (of the book) in your possession you will find the following passage: "The great-grandmother who could move tables was a Swedenborgian. She used to say to me, "After I die, listen to the wind in the trees. That's how I'll speak to you." he was a noted school teacher in San Antonio with an excellent reputation for taking a very empirical approach in her professional work. But in private she explored other domains with great panache and, in my experience, skill." "She lived to the age of 106, and after she died, I listened for her when the wind sighed in the night trees, but never heard her promised whispers, or perhaps I tuned them out." "Anne knew this statement of my gran-gran's well, so did my grandmother and my mother."

Really? I wondered, what about the specific kind of trees— i.e. pines?

I followed this apparently confirmatory email with a subsequent email and learned that both the great grandmother's home as well as Anne's and Whitley's cabin happened to be surrounded by pine trees. Hmmm....FYI, Susy Smith happened to be a Swedenborgian as well....

But it gets more interesting, as well as evidential.

It turns out that neither medium "heard" from Susy either Thursday or Friday night. However, at 5 AM on Sunday morning, one of the mediums (Suzanne Giesemann, author of many books including Messages of Hope and Wolfe's Message) was purportedly awoken by Susy and Suzanne took multiple of pages of written notes. Suzanne then carefully typed them up and gave them to Rhonda and me at noon on Sunday. The information in this reading turned out to be highly evidential. However, Susy was focused on non-Anne related material.

At one point in the reading Suzanne asked "Who is Anne?" Suzanne wrote "Nothing sensed." However, Suzanne then went on to write that: "She (Susy) draws my attention to the lower legs as if there's a challenge there such as phlebitis or neuropathy. Then she shows me someone falling or the legs taken out from under them. Not talking about herself."

Of course, lots of older people have trouble with their legs. However, the way these statements were written suggested to me that maybe this applied specifically to Anne. I then emailed Whitley and wrote "I do not know if the above issue with the lower legs applied to Anne. Might they?"

Here is what Whitley wrote back:

"Anne lost the use of her left leg due to a stroke in January of 2015. She literally fell in a coffee shop as the leg was "taken out from under" her."

This specific confirmation is compelling. Remember, at this point (1) Whitley was "blind" to (i.e. was not told) the identity of the medium, and (2) the medium was blind to (i.e. was not told) the identity of the deceased or the absent sitter, save for the first name Anne.

But it gets even more interesting and evidential. Mediums need to receive feedback about their impressions, and I felt a responsibility to share this novel confirmation from the secret grieving husband (i.e. Whitley) with Suzanne. I sent the confirmatory email on Tuesday, and Suzanne was very grateful. However, I also wrote: "Hi Suzanne - this is a follow- up to see if Susy visits you and brings Anne. If Susy shows up with Anne, please see what, if anything, Anne provides. Could be very evidential."

What happened a few hours later was super surprising.

Suzanne wrote:

"Well, that sure was interesting and unexpected. I have just finished a very strenuous workout. I sat on the couch in our bus to read emails and as I read your email the room started to go dark and I thought I was passing out. I called out to Ty and suddenly realized it was a drop-in -- it was the subject of the email. I began typing as I received impressions. They are attached. As I began typing, the symptoms eased.

"Please provide feedback."

What—a whole reading, possibly from Anne? Needless to say, I eagerly opened the attached document and noticed many items that fit Anne. The reason I now knew details about Anne was because I finished reading The Afterlife Revolution on Tuesday.

However, what mattered was how Whitley might score these items, using a rating system developed in my laboratory. Below is what I wrote to Whitley on Wednesday AM:

"Hi Whitley - see statement below from medium. It is possible that Anne showed up for the medium last night! See attached. She has no idea who you are, or Anne is. My sense is that many of the items fit Anne perfectly or very closely. I would like you to rate every possible item in the attached using the following six point scale:"

0 = The item cannot be scored (i.e. the rater does not have the necessary information to make an honest and fair rating)

1 = A clear miss (i.e. the information provided by the medium is inaccurate as applied to the particular deceased person)

2 = A stretch (i.e. the information vaguely fits the deceased)

3 = Possible fit (i.e. the information could fit the deceased)

4 = Probable fit (i.e. the information could be interpreted as being a genuine fit / hit, but it is not completely clear)

5 = A clear hit (i.e. the information can easily be scored as being accurate – i.e. the fit is obvious)

6 = A super hit (i.e. the information is especially meaningful and significant, in addition to be clearly accurate)

Besides making these 0 – 6 ratings, please provide a one sentence explanation or justification for each of the ratings. This way one can confirm that you are reliably and responsibility following the instructions and thinking through each rating.

Then, while I was waiting for a response back from Whitley, something astounding occurred that inspired me to write a separate email to Whitley (described in detail in the next section). What Whitley did was respond to this second email and include his ratings from the first email.

Here is what Whitley said:

"Wow and super-wow! I'm attaching the graded reading. I can explain them all, of course, and I have a picture of the physical bridge. She told me yesterday that this was easy for her and to "quit your caterwauling." (I was pleading with her to go to the medium.)"

What is important to share here is that there were 33 scorable items, and Whitely scored 27 (81.8 percent accuracy, conservative estimate) of them as being 5's and 6's (i.e. hits). If we add the 4 ratings of 4 (probable hits), the percent accuracy increases to 93.9 percent accuracy.

Only 2 of 33 items were scored as misses (6.1% misses /errors).

How's that for double-deceased, double-blinded accuracy?

Meanwhile, something very unexpected occurred in the feedback I received from Whitley after he formally scored the 5 AM reading. Whitley wrote: "If your medium wasn't communicating with Anne, I'll eat my Greek fisherman's cap!"

Greek fisherman's cap? Whitley was referring to sentence that I included from Suzanne's 5 AM Sunday reading with Susy which made absolutely no sense to me. Directly after the "legs taken out from under them" phrase, and "not talking about herself," Suzanne wrote:

"She's bringing my attention to a cap on Gary's head –kind of like a Greek fisherman's hat or Harley Davidson cap."

Ye, I had a Harley cap (which I rarely wear), and no, I do not have a Greek fisherman's hat. I would have rated this as a 1 or 2.

Why was Whitley referring to the Greek fisherman's hat? In a subsequent email, I asked Whitley: "do you have a Greek Fisherman's hat? That would be really weird."

Here is how Whitley responded:

"I don't have a Greek fisherman's cap, but I was with my grandson on Sunday in San Diego and he was looking at one and wanted it very much. Now he's going to get one for his birthday in a couple of weeks —from his nana! (I felt her with us, as I always do when the family is together. As she says, "I'm right here.")"

Of course, if the only evidence for Anne's presence was the coincidence between Whitley's grandson looking at Greek fisherman's hat and wanting it very much, and an evidential medium mentioning a Greek fisherman's hat when referred to Susy and Anne – as highly improbable as this pair of events is – we would not take this evidence very seriously. A skeptic would dismiss the data out of hand.

However, when (1) this highly specific and improbable evidence is combined with (2) "wind whistling," (3) "pine" trees, (4) "legs taken out from under them," all followed by (5) an entire reading containing 33 items at 81.8% accuracy (the conservative estimate), the Greek fisherman hat evidence takes on added significance and meaning, and it deserves our serious consideration (and maybe celebration?).

As you will discover as you read this book, one of the most replicated, evidential, and odd sets of evidence supporting Anne's connection with Whitley concerned the detection of a white moth by Whitley's security camera (which was recorded at the instant he was describing the phenomenon to his son a hundred miles from where it had been happening. The camera texted the image to the phone.) Whitley's description of this evidence is beautiful and stirring, and I will not reveal any more here.

However, I will mention what happened to me less than 24 hours after reading about the white moth phenomena. Below is what I wrote to Whitley:

"Thought I would give you a heads up. This morning Rhonda saw a gigantic - maybe five inch wingspan - dark moth on the ceiling of our outside porch a few feet away from our hummingbird feeder.

"Rhonda told me about it, and I requested she take a few pictures.

"I can see it right now from my home office window. I just took a few pictures for you."

We have seen such a moth maybe three times in 11 years! And I just read about the White Moth phenomena yesterday afternoon.

What are the odds?

Consider the following: how often do you (1) read about highly evidential afterlife information involving automated photographs of a white moth (or read about photographs of moths in general), and then (2) discover a super moth outside your window? FYI, I was writing the first draft of this Foreword on Wednesday afternoon, and the super moth was still there!

Was this simply a chance event, what many might interpret as a "mere" coincidence? Or, was it as Susy Smith – a journalist who wrote more than thirty books on parapsychology and life after death – of an event that was "too coincidental to be accidental", or, as Yogi Berra put it, an event that was "too coincidental to be a coincidence."?

Was this coincidence a possibly synchronicity, an event somehow mediated by Anne, or maybe mediated by something even greater? Was this a divinely inspired coincidence as Einstein described it in his famous statement, "Coincidence is God's way of remaining anonymous?"

As Whitley explains, Anne "knew" God deeply when she was in the physical, and she apparently knows even more of the reality of an all pervasive super intelligence or super mind now that she is in the greater reality. Anne's personal experiences of the divine are awe inspiring, filled with joy, friendship, and even laughter.

You are in for a special treat when you read the sections about God, plans, evolution, love, and laughter in this challenging and uplifting book.

Simply stated, the Afterlife Revolution is huge. The revolution not only involves us and our awakening here on the earth, but them and their awakening in the greater reality.

Whitley's personal journey with Anne "here" and "there" (and notice that t-here includes here) is compelling, but their integrative analysis of what is emerging and transforming both here and there is especially challenging, engaging, and enlightening.

Yes, there is much in this book to question. You will wonder how much is real and how much is imagined, just as Whitley does, and with great integrity.

I cannot underscore the question of integrity enough. Just because certain topics are unsettling if not threatening to our egos or current beliefs does not justify our ignoring or denying their potential importance. The very best evidential research mediums I have worked with (e.g. those whose average accuracy is around 90%) all speak of higher beings, include those from other planets. When we emotionally deny possible truths and dismiss them without due process or discernment, we inadvertently convert consciously intended nonfiction into unconscious fiction.

This is especially important when the ultimate take home lesson from a book is what the authors call objective love.

Here is how Anne describes it, as experienced by Whitley: "The tools that strengthen the soul – understanding and living in objective love, having a strong attention, engaging in the sensing exercise and meditation, practicing love, compassion, and humility. Those are the basics."

I have come to the conclusion that The Afterlife Revolution deserves to read, and reread. Even the ending is surprising. May you savor and learn from this book as much as I have.

Gary E. Schwartz, PhD is Professor of Psychology, Medicine, Neurology, Psychiatry, and Surgery, and Director of the Laboratory for Advances in Consciousness and Health, at the University of Arizona. His books include The Afterlife Experiments, The G.O.D. Experiments, An Atheist in Heaven (with Paul Davids), and Super Synchronicity.

CHAPTER 1

The New Revolution

IN AUGUST OF 2015, at the age of 69 and after 45 years of marriage, my wife Anne died. Not two hours after she passed away, she began a process of proving that she still exists that has changed my life completely.

For two years, she had been struggling with a catastrophic brain tumor and I had been trying with increasing desperation to save her. The dark pit of grief I fell into when I looked upon her still form was the greatest pain I had ever known.

She, however, had not been afraid to die. Ten years previously, she'd had a near-death experience that had freed her, as they do so many people who have them, from that fear.

I've never had an NDE and I was in despair. Despite all I had learned about the afterlife I feared that she was gone forever. But then, within hours of her passing, very carefully and methodically, she began to make her continued presence known.

Based on all the things about the afterlife that the two of us have learned, including some of the most extraordinary direct experiences with it ever recorded—and her return—I feel justified in saying that she still exists. I don't think we die, and I also think that we can forge a much better and more solid relationship between the physical and nonphysical sides of our species, a more reliable one than exists now.

Studies of mediums and channeling and electronic voice phenomena where conditions are created that enable those in the afterlife to express themselves in the physical world, have provided a background that strongly suggests that contact with the dead is possible, but this book is not a survey of that research. Rather, it explores the possibility of a true revolution in our relationship to reality, that emerges out of the idea that a species is not whole unless a relationship between the living and the dead is an ordinary part of life.

Over the course of this book, we will discuss certain tools that can be used to create this relationship—tools of the soul that are explained here in just this way for the first time. Then we will take a completely new look at the ageless questions of who and what we are and, above all, how to build a strong soul, lead a good life and die into joy.

While I don't expect our story to be accepted uncritically, I do want you to know that I feel sure that our book is being written by two people, one physical and one nonphysical. I am not talking to my own imagination. My wife set out to do this and she has accomplished steady, reliable communication between us, and as I think will become clear, many of the new ideas that are discussed between us in these pages emerge out of a very different perspective than we are used to in physical life.

We are calling the book the Afterlife Revolution because it is basically about making this way of living ordinary, and by doing that enabling us on the physical side to see more of ourselves and our futures, thus greatly increasing the richness of our individual lives and the capability of mankind as a whole to thrive.

It is a book, also, about replacing the fear and uncertainty that are now associated with dying with the sort of calm, informed and finally joyous attitude with which Anne and many other near-death experiencers now approach it.

It is not a lie or a hoax. It is not a cynical attempt to exploit the death of my precious wife. What I am reporting happened. On a personal level, I know it. While I cannot claim that my personal knowledge deserves to be considered universal knowledge, the evidence is strong enough that our story deserves to be taken seriously.

The experience I have had with Anne emerged out of knowledge that we gained from our relationship with the people she and I call "the visitors." They first came to our attention after I found myself face to face with them one night in late December of 1985. I later wrote the book Communion about my encounter with them. They scared me so badly that I was planning to call the book Body Terror. Anne said that it should be called Communion, because "that's what it's about." Communion with who, though—or what?

Most people who have any engagement with them assume that they are aliens from another planet. Billionaire Robert Bigelow, who has taken a longstanding interest in them, stated frankly on 60 Minutes on May 28, 2017 that they were not only aliens, but here. His company, Bigelow Aerospace, takes referrals of UFO report from the Federal Aviation Administration. He stated as well that he has had personal contact with these aliens and that he no longer cares who knows it.

I'm going to also state frankly that, while I cannot confirm that they are aliens, I have been in contact with them most of my life and have, especially in the years since Anne died, come into an intimate and ongoing personal relationship with them.

I have asked Anne about them, and she has replied that they are "inward beings."When I asked her what that meant, she said, "they live within reality. You're on the surface." I then asked, "Are they with you in your reality?" She replied, "There's only one reality. Different ways of relating to it."

I know that this sounds mysterious, but what Anne means will become clear soon enough. As matters stand, we have evolved an elaborate set of assumptions about them as aliens, right down to beliefs about the various planets they might be from and so forth—

and also the assumption that they don't exist at all, which is at least as popular. But there is something much greater, more extraordinary and far stranger going on than we have as yet realized. And also, to speak quite plainly, more wonderful.

The ones with whom we cultivated a relationship are interested in the soul, in strengthening it and in helping us create a new bond between those of us in physical life and those in the nonphysical state. In fact, this would seem to be their primary mission here, and it has become my mission, too. Anne's, too, I would think.

Had it not been for them, Anne and I would never have been able to come back into contact after her death. They taught us how. They also taught us that living as a whole species—with the physical and nonphysical sides in contact— is the next stage in evolution.

At the same time that this wonderful possibility is emerging, a sort of disease, which I think of as soul-blindness, is spreading through the human community. Ignoring the soul is a self-imposed poverty and a personal tragedy, but it is also a way of life for more and more of us every day. Souls can be nurtured and strengthened, but if their existence is denied, then that obviously cannot happen. And no matter who is here to help, they can do nothing if we ignore them and what they have to offer.

As far as the visitors who are involved in this are concerned, the soul is what matters. Everything they have taught us comes down to this: it is the soul, not the body, that is the most important part of any living creature and especially those who are like us, not only conscious but intelligent. Intelligent souls are the most creative branch of consciousness in the universe and are precious beyond belief. But not if they are confused and unformed. That's a tragedy.

Anne came to understand this deeply and became a master of the soul. It is thus her wisdom that we will communicate here, and her ideas that form the basis of the afterlife revolution.

Science in general asserts that there is no soul, and neuroscience assures us that no sign of an afterlife can be detected. Contacts with the dead are called bereavement hallucinations. As has historically been true, the scientific community is generally united in the idea that the only reality that matters is the one that can be detected by existing instruments at the present time.

In his influential book Hallucinations, Oliver Sacks discusses afterlife communications without the least thought that they may not be hallucinations at all.

Science is a great triumph of the human mind. For the past three hundred odd years, it has been applying theory to detected phenomena and coming up with ever more accurate and useful insights. But when there is data it doesn't know how to detect, the system falters.

When the great 18th century scientist Voltaire was shown fossils, he dismissed them as fish bones tossed aside by travelers. Scientists for years denied that meteors were possible because "stones cannot fall from the sky." But fossils too large to be fish bones were eventually discovered, and meteors were tracked to the ground and their celestial origin proved.

Just as Voltaire had no data to justify an investigation of fossils, science at present does not possess any data on the soul, nor any instrument that can convincingly detect it. This has led scientists to take a step too far, and assume that it doesn't exist. But what doesn't exist is not the soul, but an instrument that can detect it.

There are two impediments to the development of such a device. First, this energy—conscious energy—surely makes its own decisions about whether or not it is to be detected by instruments. Second, as scientific culture has matured, especially over the past century, an assumption has crept in that no data can exist that isn't currently detectable. So no effort to gather such data—even to understand how to go about it—is ever made. The primary focus of the scientific enterprise is no longer the search for new realities, but interpretation of the one we know now.

Science has a towering reputation. So when it makes an institutional declaration that the soul doesn't exist, even those of us who believe otherwise find ourselves doubting our own experiences of our souls and, as often as not, ending up just filtering them out.

As will be seen from some powerful examples, nonphysical

humanity very much wants contact with physical humanity. But our assumption that they don't exist creates something like a wall between us. We need to be alert to the signs that they leave in our lives. After she died, Anne went about leaving such signs for me, and did it in way calculated to defeat my inherent bias against the possibility.

Anne had read Sacks and understood the scientific view of the soul. She also felt that it was wrong. This because, after we published the book Communion about my close encounters, and letters from other witnesses around the world poured in by the tens and finally hundreds of thousands, an extraordinary secret was revealed to her that made the argument that there is no afterlife seem improbable to her. As she read and catalogued them, she came to understand the message that our visitors had left in them.

The letters and some astonishing things that happened in our lives in the early 1990s caused us to become intensely focused on the question of the afterlife.

We began to think that communication must be possible, and so started discussing what might happen when one of us died. We decided that whichever one of us moved on first would attempt contact, but not directly.

We were both too skeptical to accept something like that uncritically. So we decided that initial contacts had to be with other people who had no idea of our plan, which we never discussed with anybody.

By the time she died, though, I had forgotten all about that plan. I never dreamed that she would execute it, or even that such a thing was really possible.

When we had groups of people to our upstate New York cabin to encounter the beings who had taken an interest in us, and from the letters we received from the public, we discovered that the dead and the "visitors" as often as not appeared together.

Added to all of this came Anne's 2004 near death experience, when a stroke nearly took her life. Prior to it, she had come to accept the idea that we might in some way persist after death. Now she knew it. She had crossed over and come back.

In the end, she had become wise about the afterlife in ways I think few others have been. I can go so far as to say that Anne was probably one of the most informed experts on the subject who has ever lived, both because of all she had studied and researched, and because of personal experience.

After her NDE, she joined the larger mission of our visitors and our own dead. Her purpose was not only to show that the afterlife is real and that we need not fear death, but also that there are things we can do to prepare— not elaborate rituals, but the same straightforward, personal things that she did—that will enable us to build strong souls, communicate with our own dead while in this life, then make a good transition and be effective communicators from the other side as well.

Since her death, she has eloquently proved that the methods she advocated work.

Human beings have been trying to contact their dead for thousands of years, most recently through the use of mediums, psychics and electronic communications techniques. All would appear to work, at least at times. But personal, intimate and permanent relationships between the physical and nonphysical sides of the human family are also possible.

As we have lost touch with our souls, we have also abandoned our ancestors. But they have not abandoned us and we need them now, and more urgently than we realize, and they know it. As you will see, they have been calling to us for at least two hundred years. It is time for us to respond, and for the two sides of this family to start living and working together.

Death is not the end of anything. It is transition into a new form, just like the transformation of a caterpillar into a butterfly, and just as much part of nature. It's not supernatural, or beyond nature. There is nothing beyond nature, but there is also more to nature than we realize.

As humankind proceeds along the new path that is opening before us, we will leave our violent and anarchic history behind. Anne says that fear of death is the basis of all violence, and as we become whole as individuals, families and a species, that fear will fade away, and with it the violence that it causes.

The connection of the two halves of the species represents a turning point as fundamental as the one that caused civilization to begin and history to unfold. On this side of the change, there is one kind of history, full of blunders, confusion and terror. On the other, there emerges new sort of history altogether that is inlooking and outlooking at the same time, anchored in wonder and beckoning discovery now undreamed. It is a new way of seeing reality which brings with it a new way of being alive. In fact, it is a new birth.

After Anne died—the only woman I had ever known intimately and the absolute center of my life—I found myself drowning in a flood of grief. It buried me in such sorrow that I couldn't think, couldn't eat, could hardly move.

Parting is agony. Period. If she had come back to life in those first hours and shouted in my face, I don't think I would have heard her.

One of the first things I distinctly heard her say to me was "Grief is love in another form." I realized that when I grieved for her, I was actually loving her. Of course I grieve. I miss her at every level of my being. Even though I can communicate with her, my body misses her body so very much, and that cannot change.

Understanding this enabled me to make my grief part of my work, to respect it and love it, but also to use it to focus my attention on her presence and her words, rather than letting it bury them in my tears.

She had prepared carefully for what she knew was coming. I had, too, but not nearly as well. I so badly wanted her to stay that I could hardly think about her going, let alone in the calm, dispassionate manner with which she approached her physical end.

I didn't know it at the time, but already six months before she died, she was getting me ready to carry out my part of our mission. She did this in a characteristically subtle way, by asking me to memorize a certain poem which, as will be seen, has become central to my understanding of what she wants to do and, in fact, also central to the proof she has provided that she is still a conscious presence.

The poem, "Song of the Wandering Aengus," by W. B. Yeats, is about Aengus' lifetime of search for a "glimmering girl" who, as soon as she appeared in his life by magical means, slipped out of his arms and into a realm that might as well be called heaven.

It has become my life story, that poem of a man's search.

If ever magical means united a couple, it is what brought us together. We were two kids living in New York City who both happened to fill out the forms of a matchmaking organization. We had never known one another before. We had no mutual friends. We met on a list sent to us by the matchmakers.

From the day we sat down to lunch for the first time until the day Anne left this life, we were only once apart for as much as two weeks.

The ways in which Anne has woven that poem and its metaphors into our new life together, and done so much to prove that this new relationship is real, have granted me the most beautiful and richest experience I have ever known. I can assure you from my own life that as you come close to your dead and they to you, you will find a sweetness of the heart that you never knew was within you, and a sense of wonder that will make your life new.

But even when contact is easy and familiar, questions will and must remain—which is right and as it should be and, frankly, a big part of this whole adventure. Beliefs are walls. Questions are doors.

Despite all of our advances in knowledge, the universe still cradles the human mind in ambiguities and unknowns. We must not push them away by saying "I believe" or "I do not." Much better to abandon belief altogether, and stay with Anne's "I wonder."

Before Anne entered the nonphysical, there was one me. Now there is another, and this is not simply a grief-stricken wanderer, but a traveler on two paths at once, one in this world and one in the other.

The theme of Anne's life was joy, which she identified with acceptance of whatever happened, love for others and, above all, laughter. She would often quote that wonderful sentence of the 14th Century mystic and theologian, Meister Eckhart: "God laughs and plays." Laughter is light and as Anne understood inner search, it was about finding that light within oneself.

There are many reasons why we aren't in clear contact with the dead. One is that they are not like us. They are not unseen versions of us, but rather are living by different laws. Anne has said, "I'm not Anne anymore, I'm me. But I'll always be Anne for you, Whitley." As she describes herself and the legions of the dead, "We are an infinity of dreams." But don't be deceived. Those dreams are living presences and they are waiting for us across the bridge between our worlds. She also says, "I am the part of me that's part of you."

Those without bodies are at once more deeply individual than any physical being could ever be, but also conscious as a whole, without beginning and without end, that is outside of time and contains time. Your beloved parent, wife, child, is at once themselves as they always were, and all selves they have ever been, and all that is of being.

As a result of soul blindness, when we are facing death we use every tool we can muster to extend our lives as long as we can. When we die it is as often as not in fear and foreboding, sometimes in resignation, and those we leave behind generally never hear from us again.

This not because the dead aren't trying. When I asked Anne about this she said, "It looks as if you're intentionally ignoring us." And that is exactly what we are doing. We're hypnotized by the physical, by which I mean that we are looking so intently into material reality that we simply cannot see beyond it.

She says "The first time you ignored me, I was upset. Then I got mad at you. I yelled. You acted as if I didn't exist. It was weird and confusing."

We have come a long way together since those early struggles. I know how to listen for her now and how to let her into me. Her communications are fleeting, identifiable to me by a sense of the unbidden and a taste of her presence. I keep a notebook with me now all the time, because I know that I will forget her words after they fly past, often in seconds. This, I think, is because they are not my thoughts, not part of my mind, and have no place to land in my brain. Like flashes on the wing of a passing bird, they are there then gone.

They leave behind two things: wonder and questions. Always Anne's beloved questions. Communion, would not have ended with the group of questions that it did had it not been for Anne's influence.

As she read my manuscript, she would say again and again, "Whitley you don't know that. Rewrite it as a question."

The great human question is "will I live on after death?" It is simple, universal and haunts us all, every one, all the time. Science, by insisting with such compelling authority that we are mortal flesh and no more, reinforces our fear of annihilation. At the same time, the increasingly complex and vivid material world makes it harder and harder for us to hear the soul's subtle inner voice.

But even as many of us are giving up on the soul, the voices of many others are being raised, proclaiming that there is indeed an afterlife. In 2011, researcher Pim Van Lomel, writing in the Annals of the New York Academy of Sciences reported that nine million people in the United States alone have reported near death experiences. Anne was such a person, and like very many of them returned to this life with no fear of death. Like most, she was brought back by medical science.

How ironic that the same science that is telling us that the soul doesn't exist is also responsible for one of the foundations of the afterlife revolution.

Over the course of our narrative, Anne will describe her new life in ways that seem to me to be revelatory. She was highly articulate, and brings her descriptive skills to bear in her depiction of what it is like to be on her side of the divide. But don't expect simple stories of loving light. The world she describes is a complex place full of nuance and ambiguity, and it is also very surprising.

Among the most surprising things about it is that, when you die into it, you're not surprised. We are much more nonphysical beings than we are physical. These journeys through time that we take by entering bodies are valuable but brief. Most of our experience is not physical at all.

Once a new and more reliable means of contact becomes commonplace, as it will, then this species is going to wake up to its true reason for existence, and in so doing is going to reach a whole new level of life. There is joy ahead in the afterlife revolution, but joy

11

requires a light approach. As Anne puts it, "the hardest thing to do is to let this be fun. But once you do, then it's easy."

When, soon after I had the December 26, 1985 close encounter that would lead to the writing of Communion, I told her what I thought had happened to me, she went right to the heart of the matter: 'let's figure this out, we'll do it together, and what an adventure!'

I had feared that she might want to divorce her crazy husband to protect her child from his ravings, but that could not have been further from the truth. From the first days, before we knew anything except that something had really shaken me up, she was right there beside her man with support, guidance and, above all, insight and, frankly, excitement. She was definitely up for that adventure.

Her thinking is reflected in every word I have written about the phenomenon. In fact, it is the foundation of my work. Over the years, working together, we learned a great deal from our visitors, about them, and about the human journey. Anne, especially, understood that they had aspirations for us and what those aspirations were, and their motives for revealing themselves not only to me and us, but to so many people worldwide.

I think that their greatest hope is that we become rich, strong souls and that our species survives and evolves for a long time to come.

Their message about what we need to do in order to achieve this new sort of enrichment is clear. To experience the true richness of our humanity, we need to be a species united.

This is the afterlife revolution, a journey into a new evolution of mankind and an entirely new experience of living.

But how? How do we recover our contact not only with our own souls but with those who have already passed out of the flesh? Where are they? What do they want and need from us? What is on offer from them?

Anne has executed a plan that we laid years ago that has proved to me that she still exists. She has done it on behalf of the great mission of which she is now a part, to make this species whole in an entirely new way. But why has she been able to do this? Is there something about her that give her a special ability, or is she simply using a skill that is part of every human soul, and teaching me on my side of the bridge how to use it, too?

We will explore these things together, and show just how the skill we are using works and can work in any life and any relationship. Establishing the bridge between the worlds means a more competent, more peaceful and happier species.

Working together across the bridge between the worlds, Anne and I vote for this future. Of course there are challenges now, with all the changes that are taking place on planet Earth. But we have glimpsed the possibilities and they are more marvelous by far than even our most optimistic speculations.

We are under pressure now from circumstances that would be familiar to our distant ancestors. They, also, struggled through hard times to reach a new life. A hundred thousand years ago, when the world entered the last ice age, they were naked wanderers. When it ended, they had learned to clothe themselves, they had language, they were organized into tribes and expert in everything they needed for survival.

Once again, we are going to find our way into a new life— but this time, it will be truly new, for we are going to learn to live at once in and beyond the material world, moving into an expansive reality that is just now beginning to reveal itself to us. To reach this new mankind, whole at last, there is also coming a new journey.

That journey is what this book is about.

CHAPTER 2

The Shadow Falls

AS MY BRILLIANT, deeply thoughtful wife gazed into a personal distance, she said quietly, "Whitley, it's time."

I wanted so badly to ask her, "time for what?" I wanted her to mean that she was looking toward some further episode in our life together. But that wasn't it, and I knew it. Her tumor had not grown since her surgery two years before, but the part that had to be left behind was now stressing her brain's vascular system. The doctors had warned us that the strokes she was having would get worse.

A few days before, her left side had become much weaker. Her future was grim: more strokes until she died. The great danger was that she would become unable to communicate before that happened and be forced to die a lingering, helpless death, maybe suffering pain she could not communicate.

Our life together had been a subtle, intricate dance of mutual discovery and a joy greater than any I could have imagined before meeting this complex and yet welcoming human being.

Many times before, I had talked her out of it, pleading with her to stay a little longer. I had done everything I could to give her a rich life experience despite the cancer and the growing paralysis.

We had often spoken together about end-of-life. She had researched her situation carefully and prepared her plan in such a way that she could depart from the world with dignity and in an entirely legal manner.

Depart from me, she who was more than half of me.

She had said the previous January that she had prayed that the stroke that had paralyzed her left side then would take her. But instead it left her unable to rise from a chair, to use her left arm, to read, even to see well enough to watch television. While her mind was as acute as ever, her eyes and ears could not make sense of the world around her. She had become a brilliant presence trapped behind a wall of defective sensory input.

I read to her, explained things to her, kept her abreast of world events. Because just moving her from bed to chair was so exhausting, we hired helpers to ease our days. I found things she could enjoy, even things as simple as going out to get an ice cream, and I made sure that her life was as rich as it could be. Despite the difficulty, we went to the movies, the theater, had dinners out, went to a weekly reading group we both loved—in short, kept up with our life as best we could.

When she couldn't put things together, I explained them to her later, and we managed to make those conversations a lot of fun for us both.

She participated with enthusiasm, as she did in rehabilitation and physical therapy. But there was that tumor mass remaining, and its presence prevented any progress with rehab. In the months between January and July, she went to therapy three times a week but got essentially nowhere.

When she experienced the increase in weakness, I suggested that we go to the hospital to see if she was having another stroke. But she was finished with hospitals.

She was as bright as ever, as wonderful as ever, full of joy, wisdom and humor. She was not afraid. On the contrary, she was calm and

15

practical. On a day in early August, she told me that, starting the next morning, she was going to carry out her end of life plan, which was to refuse food and drink.

I had tried so hard to prevent this moment from coming. But also there was a part of me that was so very tired that the idea of not living in this haze of work seemed freeing—which only added an element of guilt to my grief. I wanted her to stay, but I knew that I wasn't making it, either. My left knee was destroyed from lifting. My back hurt all the time. To keep going I had to spend my nights on ice packs. I was at the chiropractor twice a week, sometimes more often. I couldn't write, so we were in yet another dangerous financial spiral.

The truth was that her illness had exhausted us both. I would see her watching me as I worked to lift her, to cook, clean and so forth. Even with help, I was running out of steam and she knew it.

Because she couldn't travel, we could no longer see our grandchildren except on the rare occasions that they could visit us. She felt that we were valuable to them. "Whitley, we know some of the deepest secrets about life that there are. We need to pass that down." This was much on her mind. She knew that, if she saved one of us, then at least they would have that benefit.

I had told her that, when she went, I wanted to go, too. I am no more afraid of death than she was.

She insisted I stay behind for the kids, and to complete this book. I had to agree and now I'm sure this was the right thing to do. In a deep way, in the part of life we never see, she both lived as she did and gave up her life for her mission. I am grateful and proud that she entrusted me with completing it. I can only hope that my effort is adequate to the task set me.

On that first night of her dying, I sat beside her as she lay sleeping. But I was unable to stop crying and had to leave the room so she wouldn't wake up to that. What she was doing was as hard a thing as a person can experience. I did not want to make it even harder for her, so she did not need to see my own agony.

I hoped that morning would bring a change of mind. But when she woke up, she was even more determined. Finally, my heart just broke and I cried openly. I couldn't help it. She touched me gently on the cheek and said, "What would my life have been worth if there was nobody to grieve for me?"

Then I was glad she saw my pain, and my grief just poured out of me. The harder I tried to choke it back, the more intense it became. She stroked my head with her good hand, and simply let it happen. She didn't cry. I wouldn't have either if I'd been in her shoes. Her decision was a hard one, but for her also a relief.

Just as she was not afraid, she was not sad. Instead, the most conscious human being I had ever encountered, my beloved wife, was deeply and profoundly ready.

All morning we talked quietly together, side by side in our chairs. The healthcare aides came and went. We said nothing to them of Anne's decision. Instead, we reminisced about a life filled with wonderful moments. I remembered her coming down the aisle in the Lady Chapel at the back of St. Patrick's in New York, lovely in blue and with wine red roses at her waist. It wasn't exactly a big wedding. We only had two hundred dollars. There were some friends there, a beloved cousin and her husband, my mother, a priest and a sleepy altar boy. But it was the most wonderful day of our lives.

Our best friends had come up from Washington. They couldn't afford a hotel, so we ended up spending our wedding night in our tiny apartment with them camped out in the living room. We didn't care. We were so happy.

Then came seven long years of struggle to sell a book and establish me as a writer. Anne became my muse and editor. She went back to school and got a degree in English Literature to make herself better at both.

Occasionally, I would give up, clear my desk and put my typewriter out with the trash. Inevitably, the next afternoon when I returned from work, everything would be back in its place, often with notes from Anne about how to move ahead with whatever story I was writing. Finally after half a dozen novels and hundreds of rejections, the Wolfen sold. Anne got pregnant at once and the next thing we knew, we had a book in the stores and a baby in the house. (We now had two bedrooms.)

It was all so hard and such fun. And discovering one another as people, too, that was such a joy.

Anne had an oppressed childhood. She'd had to keep her mouth shut and endure whatever was dished out to her. Her opinions had not been wanted and her feelings had not mattered. Now, in a new relationship, I think that she was wondering if things had changed. I loved her, she knew that, but could I bear her?

She set out—not quite consciously, I wouldn't think—to test this.

In our first months together, I could see her suppressing her anger. I didn't often make her mad, but it was a new relationship and there were inevitable moments of friction. Any anger or disappointment she might feel she covered with smiles.

When I saw that, I would say, "Have I made you mad?" She'd say no. Then I would laugh and her lips would tighten.

Eventually, what I was instinctively probably hoping would happen did: all the suppressed annoyances and irritations boiled over and she blew up in my face. It came after I kept saying that I wanted to return to London, where I had lived the year before I met her.

She cried out, "So go! Leave! Get out of my life!" And then she burst into tears. And so did I. But that didn't end it. Fury had erupted in her, but her eyes were filled with fear. She raged on, out of control, terrified that she was driving me away but unable to contain her anger.

This was a person who did not consider that she had a right her own feelings, not to her anger or her happiness, or to love and be loved, any of it.

She screamed at me to leave right now so she didn't have to look at me anymore. Coming from a family where voices were rarely raised, I was deeply shocked. But I also saw that she had been stifled and pushed aside for a long time.

I decided that she would not have the experience of having to stifle her feelings again, not ever. She had a man and this man treasured her, and her anger was important to him— and she had a right to fully express it and to have her needs understood and respected. She had been a sort of throwaway. Not now. Now, Anne mattered.

I told her that she had become part of my heart and I wanted to be part of hers. I needed her and could not live without her.

She looked at me like I had just arrived from Mars. I said, "Forgive me honey, I was insensitive. If anybody goes to London, it has to be both of us." Then I took her in my arms. She opened the door to herself much wider then, and our love affair flowered.

Once she realized that fits of temper weren't going to drive me off, she did a lot of exploding. I think that I experienced every temper tantrum in her life that she'd had to suppress before we met. Once, she got so loud that the neighbors called the police. She proceeded to hide and I was left to explain to six cops that she was actually OK even though she refused to make an appearance.

The fights always ended with us throwing ourselves into each other's arms, and then going on from there. And gradually, she learned to complain when an annoyance was small rather than waiting until it filled her with rage. She became good at what is now called anger management, and our relationship settled into one of quiet mutual respect and enjoyment of one another. The loving acceptance that had replaced all the fireworks enabled the relationship to deepen even more. We didn't know it, but our souls had come together. The inner marriage—modeled in the esoteric practice of Alchemy as the chemical wedding—had taken place, and we would now live and grow together as one. Truly we were married.

There was much beauty in our relationship and much fun, and also much humor. We ended up spending most of that last day of our life together in this world laughing over things that had amused us in the past, me through my tears, her with deep and genuine pleasure.

After refusing food and drink all day, I knew that she was now hungry and thirsty. I asked her "Would you like supper?"

She smiled gently. "No, baby," she said. Then she added, "Whitley, it's time for hospice. I need them here in the morning."

OK, so this was it. She was committed, at least for now. I'd waited for her to get good and hungry and good and thirsty. But she wasn't going to break her fast. Instead, she was ready to brave a night of hunger pangs and thirst.

I could not let her go through that. We'd already chosen our hospice. They knew her situation and her plan, and were ready to come when called.

I made the hardest telephone call of my life. I'd been dreading it for months. I could barely talk. But I manage to get it out: it was time. Anne was fasting.

They came at about nine that evening and began giving her the assistance that was then allowed by law, consisting basically of mild doses of morphine to relieve her discomfort, and a mouth lubricant.

The next morning when the registered nurse came, the first order of business was for me to leave the house so that she could ask Anne without me present whether or not she wanted to continue, and if she understood clearly that this would cause her death. So far, she had been given only one light dose of morphine. Her mind must not be clouded, I'd made sure of that. There must be no mistakes here. To keep her comfortable, I'd stayed up all night making sure that she would have mouth lubricant and chapstick the instant she called for them.

I drove around aimlessly, struggling to see the streets through my tears.

When I returned, I could see from the grave expression on the nurse's face what Anne's answer had been.

Nevertheless, every two hours until she lost consciousness, I asked her again if she wanted to change her mind. I wanted so badly to beg but I forced myself not to. She saw my tears and my great anguish. I could not hold that in, and it was plea enough.

On the Friday before she died, there was a ray of hope. She said that she wanted to go to the movies. She wanted popcorn and a coke. My heart leaped and I said "Sure, let's do it." But then I had to add, "You're too deep in the fast to just

break it. We'll need a couple of days for you to come back." I had researched this whole process with the utmost care. I knew exactly what would be required at any point in the fast to bring her back, and when that would no longer be possible.

She smiled softly and said, "No, I'd just have to do it all over again."

Even so, I can't put to rest the idea that, if I'd just been a little more convincing, a little more hopeful, she might have ended the fast.

But she was right. If she'd returned from it, she would only have decided to do it again. I had no right to wish that on her and I'm glad now that she stuck to her decision.

She could not get better and she could easily have come to a point where she could no longer make decisions. Then the legal situation would have become much more complicated. The Supreme Court has ruled that a person of sound mind has an absolute right to refuse food and drink, but not that a family member can make such a decision for a loved one who is unable to communicate.

This way, she kept her dignity and approached death in full consciousness.

We'd discussed the morphine dosing very carefully with our doctor. She wanted to have a conscious experience of dying. I wanted her to remain aware of what she was doing as long as possible on the chance that she might yet change her mind.

I know that she made the right decision and was right to stick to it. But that didn't mean that I wouldn't suffer terribly and experience extraordinary mental anguish. I did and still do and always will, and that's how it should be. She was more valuable to me than I am to myself, and so of course the grief of loss is and will remain part of me. I remember the last time I said to her, "Anne, refusing food and water means that you're going to die. Do you want to change your mind?"

There was no answer. Her eyes were closed. She had slipped into the deep, last sleep that would soon become a terminal coma.

Anne had left—sort of.

Within hours, she would begin to communicate telepathically—and for those of you who scoff at that, please try to keep an open mind or, barring that, put our book aside. Our story is not for you. But for those of you who will at least entertain such things as a possibility, do read on because a great story is going to be told here, of a love that has survived death and a marriage that is still flourishing even though one of the partners no longer has a physical presence in the world. It is a universal story, too, told in many different lives, but in the privacy of the home and the silence of the heart. Here, it is going to unfold on the page.

My grief is about the loss of her body, not the absence of her being. In fact, as you will see over the course of our story, in her new state Anne has become a presence of great intelligence, compassion and, above all, insight.

By Monday morning, she was completely silent. I was in the most powerful emotional state not only that I had ever known, but that I had ever known was possible. It was not anguish only, but anguish mixed with something close to awe.

I was aware that I was witnessing the departure of a great soul.

She'd started out in life in the most humble of circumstances. To her schoolmates, as they had written to me when I contacted a few of them, she'd seemed to be a quiet, ordinary girl. Nobody had ever bothered to nurture her mind. Until I met her, her brilliance hadn't mattered to anyone. All it had meant in her life was that she was constantly annoying people by correcting them. Because she was a natural teacher, she could not resist explaining to people better ways of doing things. This was resented, and she used to get fired every few months.

She hadn't the slightest idea how bright she was. But I knew within ten minutes of meeting her, as the brilliant thoughts and insights poured out of her and her sharp wit sparkled, that I had a treasure. I had wanted a smart wife. Very smart. As smart as possible. By the time we'd known each other for a week, I was aware that she was the brightest person I'd ever met, and I was determined that, if the relationship worked, the first thing on the agenda was to get her the education she deserved.

When I would look into her bright brown eyes, I saw not just a twenty-two year old girl. I could see a being of great depth hiding behind that innocent sparkle. I wanted the girl in my life, but I wanted that other person, too, the genius who was hiding inside, peeking out uneasily at me, afraid she'd drive me off.

From that day to this, I have lived in the shadow of a hidden master, whose wisdom and strength towered above my own. I have loved every minute of this great privilege, and I still do.

I was going to miss her sweet presence and enormous mind more than I thought it would be possible to bear, but I also knew that she was going forth in triumph, for she had done things in this world that were marvelous, but at the same time had remained gentle and humble. She knew how extraordinary her insight into the close encounter experience had been, but she did not wear that or any of her other accomplishments like a badge, and she did not resent the dismissive ways of the world. She didn't like the way we were treated, of course, but instead of wrapping herself in anger and resentment, she simply continued with her work

Those early struggles with anger management had made her skillful at accepting injustice and disappointment.

I remember when we were watching the first episode of South Park together and realizing that it was a lampoon of me, she took my hand and said to me, "They're empty people and they know it and you're not and they know that, too, and that makes them mean."

She knew people and she knew me, I think, better than I knew myself.

As we always had, on our last night together we slept side by side and hand in hand. When I squeezed her hand during the night, I thought perhaps she squeezed back, so I spent the day reading poems to her that we loved, Whitman's "There was a Child Went Forth," Wordsworth's "Ode on Intimations of Immortality Recollected from Early Childhood," Eliot's "Waste Land," Lowell's "Skunk Hour." I read Ecclesiastes and Molly Bloom's Soliloquy from "Ulysses" and many of the couplets from Joe Brainerd's "I Remember." And, most especially, of course, "Song of the Wandering Aengus."

Anne's first moment of telepathy came when she was in her final coma. She had been unconscious for about four hours when one of our caregivers suddenly said, "She just told me she wants to die in red

23

pajamas!" The woman was so absolutely certain that this request had really come from Anne that she instantly leaped up and ran out to a department store and got some. We dressed my wife's thin, faded body in them.

Note here how certain the woman was and how that motivated her. It was just like being spoken to by somebody who was alive, and yet it wasn't a voice like a radio or anything like that. It was what I have come to think of as a "silent voice," a sort of knowing what is being said without hearing anything. It is not, in other words, an auditory hallucination. Instead, it's a spontaneous inner speaking that carries with it the flavor of another personality. When it is strong and quick and not of yourself, it is hard to mistake.

Anne's choice of the color red was no accident. She was already living partly in the world of the dead and partaking of the knowledge that is there.

She has since taught me how colors reflect different vibrations of light and different levels of being, and shown me the colors that are associated with the body and the soul and their commingled relationship. She says, "Paint fades, but color is immortal." The body dies, but the soul persists.

To understand the significance not only of colors but also of many other messages from those in nonphysical reality, it is important to know the principle of the triad. A triad has three sides: active, passive and harmonizing.

Because the body is the active side of the triad of being, its color is red. One can easily sense how red suggests urgency and action, just as green does passivity and peace. She wanted to leave this world symbolically clothed in the color of blood and life.

By the evening of Tuesday, August 11, 2015, Anne's coma had reached its terminal phase. She lay in our bed, in the spot where I now sleep every night and from where I hope one day to leave, also.

My son and daughter in law had come up that morning. It was clear that the end was near. The three of us were in the dining area when I heard Anne say in my mind, "Whitty, I'm dying right now."

I leaped up and rushed into the bedroom and lay beside her. I put my hand on her chest and felt the beat of her heart. I said, "goodbye, goodbye, goodbye." As I spoke, her heart stopped.

My center, more of me than I am, had left her body—and me —behind.

Despite all I had already seen of those in the afterlife and all we had both learned about nonphysical consciousness, in that moment it felt as if she was gone forever.

Never one to waste time, however, she was prompt to make her continued existence known. It wasn't a fleeting thing, either. From a small beginning on that first night, it has grown into a relationship that is, if anything, even richer and more complex than it was when we both had bodies. The sweetness of the flesh is missing, of course, but it has been replaced by a commingling of being that is the deepest companionship that I think I could ever know.

Anne and I live, now, facing one another across the bridge of love. I go to her side sometimes but we the living cannot stray far from our bodies. More often, she comes to me.

In this life, Anne was wise. Now she is profoundly so. She was intelligent. Now her mind glows with brilliance.

After she died, I lay beside her with my hand still on her chest. I was unable to move. I fought for breath. Then I heard her say, "Get up, go on."

I could practically feel her pushing at me. I sensed that she was very close. Finally I got up and sat beside her. We called the nurse, who came in about half an hour and confirmed that she had passed.

There she lay, a ruin. My God. She had given so much of value to this world and had been so ignored during her life. Just as I had seen her from the first for what she was, I saw her contribution for what it is, which is a fundamental discovery about the nature of humanity and our place in the universe. As we shall see, what she learned and taught—and is teaching right now—not only identifies our place in the world, it also tells us why this strange experience we call life even happens.

Soon after her death was officially confirmed, two people from the medical school arrived to take her body. She had bequeathed it to the medical students so that, even in death, it would continue to be the vessel of a teacher.

That was very hard for both me and my son. The idea that she would be dissected instead of buried or cremated in the presence of those who loved her was so very, very hard to bear. But it was her wish and, as with almost everything our gentle teacher did, also a lesson on many different levels, not least among them that we should not let ourselves be attached to the physical form.

As in many other spiritual disciplines, there is in the Gurdjieff Work, which we joined in 1970 and which continues to play a big part in my life, an idea called "identification." We identify with who and what we love, and in so doing lose track of our own true selves.

Anne was an expert on identification. She would never speak of it overtly, but when she saw an identification, she was quick to challenge it. So I understood that she was not only donating her body for the sake of the medical students, but to give my son and me the chance to see our identification with her physical form and free ourselves from it.

The flesh is not what matters, and she had finished using her body. The best thing that could be done now was to let it be used to teach others. And so, in fulfillment of her wish, that's exactly what was done.

I had promised of who were sitting together in vigil that I would let them know when she died, and at 7:45 PM I texted them the news. One of them, Leigh McCloskey, opened Ranier Maria Rilke's "Letters on Life" at random. His eyes rested on page 121, and this is what he read:

"In life there is death and it astonishes me that everyone claims to ignore this fact: there is death, the pitiless presence of which we are made aware with every change that we survive because one must learn to die slowly. We must learn how to die: there is all of life. To prepare from afar the masterpiece of a proud and supreme death, of a death where chance does not play a role, of a death that is well wrought, quite happy, of an enthusiasm that the saints had known how to achieve' the masterpiece of a long-ripened death that effaces its odious name by restoring to the anonymous universe the recognized and rescued laws of an intensely accomplished life."

He found this passage at random, or perhaps not. Perhaps Anne opened it for him and through him. The reason I say that is that, just a few minutes later, perhaps ten minutes after her death, I found a book fallen open in our office. It was Roy Frieden's Physics from Fisher Information and it was laid open to a page on which Anne had years before marked the sentence "...a single observation of the metric occurred at the onset of the Universe, and this generated the Wheeler-DeWitt equation for the pure radiation universe which had existed then. In other words, the gravitational structure of the Universe was generated out of a single, primordial quest for knowledge." (Like Bohm's "pilot waves," the Wheeler-Dewitt equation is an attempt to reconcile Einsteinian relativity with quantum indeterminacy.)

I asked everybody in the house whether or not they'd taken the book down in the last few minutes, because it had been on the shelf untouched for years.

They had not.

I was reminded of a remarkable story which a famous surgeon had told me, about how he had been given all the details of an important surgery he had developed. (It's not in his biography, so I'm leaving his name out. In this strange world of ours, the story would diminish the reputation of a fine man who deserves all the honor that his life accorded him.) He was in the hospital suffering from an infection of the myocardial sac. He'd gone into crisis and began calling for the nurses, but none came. However, a woman in a long white gown suddenly glided into his room, plunged her hands into his chest, then glided out. In that instant, the entire design of the surgery he pioneered came into his mind. Moments later, the nurses rushed in, explaining that they'd been in the next room because the patient, an older woman, had just died. He felt that his surgery had come into his mind because of what that woman's departing soul had done.

Anne loved the story and we discussed it often. So it was logical that she would leave behind a crucial piece of information as she departed. She knew that I would understand.

Later that night, at 9:20, she had just been taken away and for the first time in all these years, my life was empty of her. I was sitting alone, bereft, and asking her if she still existed, and if so, would she somehow contact me. I was asking her with carefully structured intensity in my inner voice. A moment later, my phone rang. It was another dear friend, Belle Fuller, saying that she'd just that moment had a message from Anne to call me. I was so grateful and surprised that I almost couldn't reply. It was a lovely moment. She'd had no idea that Anne had just died.

As the little van had rolled away down our alley with that beloved body inside, a peculiar sort of mist appeared. I took a photo of the van as it left, its brake lights glowing amid many colors in the strange, soft haze. The photo, taken at night, doesn't show the colors that could be seen, but the mist is clearly visible.

As it turned out, that mist was the first manifestation of something that is known to happen when certain souls pass from this life. The Tibetans call such souls "rainbow bodies." There will often also be rainbows, and as I drove to Anne's wake a few days later, rainbow after rainbow appeared. I also took pictures of them as my son and I drove along.

Anne would laugh to hear herself called a great soul, but that's exactly what she is, and not only that, she is still very much turned toward this world. The reason, I feel sure, is the mission she is on. Beyond our current reality, there is a new humanity. We are one half of it, still darkly afraid and confused, living in what Anne calls "the level of violence." The other half awaits, its arms open, to welcome us at last into the union that is our destiny.

CHAPTER 3

A Flash of Light

ABOUT THREE HOURS after her death, I saw Anne in my mind's eye. She was walking toward me. She was moving carefully, as she had not been able to walk for half a year. But she was there, definitely walking, and by grace and her love showing me that she could do so once again. As I looked at her, I saw that her eyes had changed. Rather than the bright softness of life, they were penetrating and intense. They were the eyes of knowledge, but also in them was a sparkle of something that seemed to me to be satisfaction. She looked like a victor, radiant. It was as if the wonderful twinkle of life had become a great, sounding chorus of purest joy.

The tears poured down my face.

That night, I did not think I would sleep. How could I? The emptiness of our bed was horrifying. Anne's death was incredible. Unbelievable. And yet, instead of lying there in tears as I had expected, I fell at once into a deep sleep. It was almost like an enchanted sleep, it was so deep.

Then I saw her, still dressed as she had been when she walked toward me. She turned and gave a little wave. Wherever she was, she was moving up and away from me, and fast.

I knew instantly what I wanted to do, which was to accompany her as far as I could go. I'd read the Tibetan Book of the Dead and thought not only from its descriptions of the region between death and life, but from my own experiences, that the first part of the journey Anne was starting could be confusing and unsettling. If I could, I wanted to help and protect my beloved.

Usually, I cannot leave my body by my own efforts. I must be taken out. But this time I moved out easily, slipping into the layer of life that lies just above the physical world.

We soared out into a region that seemed almost like it was under water. Shadowy enormous forms loomed around us, watching us alertly. Then we broke into the sweetest light I have ever known, moving faster and faster, farther and farther. Anne was laughing a bit at my persistence, but I would not go away—until, finally, I was caught short by the cord that connects the soul to the body. She rose away from me, gazing back, smiling, and then was gone.

And then I was back in the bed alone.

I gave voice to my grief, stifling my anguished howls in my pillow so I wouldn't disturb the neighbors. But then I slept again. It felt as if a kind hand had been laid on my head, her hand, in such peace and in such love as I had never and yet had always known, for it was greater than normal, physical love. It was the calm and accepting love of one soul for another, what Anne calls "objective love."

 In her diary on Unknowncountry.com, in an entry dictated to me on July 10, 2017, she said, "I no longer experience subjective, or sentimental, love. I am in love with reality. I am part of the joy of consciousness. I am me and all being both at the same time. Objective love is the energy that created the universe and that sustains its expansion. There is a quest for knowledge going on. Everything seeks to be known. This desire is objective love. It loves all knowledge, not just the things that are pleasant or nice. It loves and desires the dark, too."

It is also the key to building the bridge between the worlds. But before that was going to happen, continued efforts had to be made to get me to understand and take action.

The next afternoon, a Wednesday, I received an email from a friend in Florida, author Trish MacGregor. Trish and her husband and co-author Rob had gotten word from a mutual friend that Anne had died, and I had written them to let them know that it had been a peaceful passing. While Trish was writing back, what she describes in her blog as "an incredibly strange thing" happened. As she was typing "Thank you for letting us know that she died peacefully. If we can do anything to help out, in any way, please let us know," there was what she describes as "a brilliant flash of light and a huge explosion" in their house. At first they were terrified, then puzzled to discover that nothing had exploded. The house was fine. The explosion took place just as Trish typed the last "know." She says in her blog, "We think it was Anne, making her presence known." Given all that has happened, I would say that this could well be the case. But it worried me, of course. Had Anne's death been harder than it had seemed to me? Was she angry or upset? She had seemed so at peace right after her passing. Maybe it was a burst of joy affirming Trish's comment. That's what Trish thought and what I hope, but I could not know and I cannot know.

The death of one so beloved leaves a great wound, but not knowing if she really wanted to do what she did, if she perhaps changed her mind after she could no longer speak, if she suffered but could not say it—all of these doubts and fears are mine to bear. When I heard Trish's words, I remembered Anne's temper, and how I was often responsible for her anger. Was this true now?

A great part of the journey of grief is learning to let such doubts go. There is nothing more to be done. She has entered a new reality and I cannot bring her back, not to touch and hold. But I can communicate with her, so I asked her why she had done what she did to Trish. She said, "Because it was fun."

At first, of course, I was delighted with the answer. It was so like Anne.

But there was seriousness, too. It was important to Anne that Trish notice and that she communicate her experience. It might have been fun to do, but it also guaranteed that notice.

It was about that time that I remembered our plan from so many years ago. The one to die first would initiate communication through friends, not directly.

I thought, 'my God, she's doing it!'

Although I cannot pinpoint an exact time or specific perception that took me beyond the amazement factor into assuming Anne's continued presence, it was during this period that I started to think more deeply about the mission. She wasn't just trying to contact me to be nice to her husband, she was doing it for a reason. In her own way, as articulate as always, she was taking up the cause of the afterlife revolution.

Her efforts to prove her existence by contacting people other than me continued. I had not only never told anybody about our plan, I hadn't thought of it myself in years, not until I realized what she was doing.

At six o'clock on the morning after her death, a filmmaker of our acquaintance, Alex Rotaru, found himself waking up quite suddenly. It was unusual for him to awaken at that early hour. He immediately felt the presence of Anne all around him. She said, "I have lots of ideas." In the next moment, he found the way to end a film he has been struggling with for two years. He has a lot of it shot, but has been unable to come up with the ending. In this life, she'd been concerned about the fact that he was stuck. Now, from the next, she gave him what he needed.

Anne's next moment of contact was the one that made me all but certain that she was executing our plan.

I needed to get out of the house and not be alone, so my kids proposed a visit to the desert city of Palm Springs. Anne and I had spent many lovely weekends in the desert, so I thought it would be an ideal getaway. I would be out of the house, but in a place we had both loved.

On the afternoon of our first day there, we drove into the mountains above the small city. My kids decided to go hiking. I could not follow them because my bad knee would never take the strain. So I sat on a bench and waited for them to return.

I spoke in my mind to Anne, asking once again for some sort of sign that she still existed. Within seconds, my cellphone rang. Although I was in a pretty isolated area, it turned out that cell coverage was more or less normal. I answered it to find a good friend from Nashville on the other end. This was Clare Henry, the wife of author William Henry. She said, "Whitley I just had a message from Anne. She said to call you and tell you she was all right."

Then I knew. This could not be a coincidence. In fact, it was not just a perfectly timed call, it was also the only time that Clare had ever telephoned me. I made a decision. Anne had proved to me that she was still here. She not only still existed, she was conscious and aware of what was going on in my mind, and had new powers of communication.

Right now it feels as if we are sitting side by side, the way we used to when we worked. She says, "Except what I have to offer now is different. It's accurate vision."

Our species, in this time of crisis, certainly needs that. She adds, "but don't forget to say that it has limitations. The future isn't an open book to us, but it's also not a complete unknown. We see more clearly because we can tell the difference between the inevitable, the probable, the possible and the impossible. There's no guesswork."

Such insight will be a significant advance over what those of us on the physical side of the species have now. But when it comes to communication between the two sides, objectivity and repeatability are necessary, otherwise we end up with nothing but guesswork, confusion and runaway imagination. Anne says, "Numbers are essential. A lot of you need to be able to cross the bridge in order to detect any consensus we come up with." I would also add that consistency of response is what we should look for. I can envision a situation where many people, working together in an organized manner with each other and their beloveds on the other side could build an exchange about the future that would be consistent enough to be actionable.

WHITLEY AND ANNE STRIEBER

More than that, though, the new relationship is going to be about the enrichment of souls on both sides of the bridge. For that's what life is about. It is about the soul. And the universe, all of it. It is about the soul.

As we build our bridges and seek to make our species whole, we will need to understand what is a belief and thus open to question, and what is knowledge, and thus actionable.

All these events—Belle's call followed by Clare's, Trish and Rob's experience, Alex's dream—caused me to alter my basic question about whether or not Anne's consciousness was still intact. This was no longer a speculation, but a possibility. But knowledge? Was my expectation that Anne still existed now knowledge, at least for me?

I decided that I should do what I could to draw more confirming events. Whereupon Anne said, "Fine, but don't get stuck."

One of the hardest things about being in contact with the dead is believing that it's real. This is because we determine reality based on physical cues, and they are totally absent in this type of communication. So we want signs, sign after sign.

I am no different. As soon as one sign appears, I'm looking for another. We were in continuous communication for 45 years, talking, touching, loving—being physically together in every way. Not a day passes that my body is not startled anew by her absence. And yet my mind knows that she's here. Right now, this moment. Here. I hear her speak to me, see various manifestations, get convincing reports from others that are so varied and consistent that they qualify as personal knowledge. Not universal knowledge, certainly, but on a personal basis, yes.

However, my body's reaction is different. Without smells, tastes, sounds—no physical manifestations at all, as far as it's concerned—she's gone. Unlike my mind, it has no way of believing otherwise. As it no longer has any confirmation of her existence, it adds a layer of question—which is good. Far better to open the door with question than close it with belief. Above all, we must not look to those in the nonphysical as prophets and guides.

The reason for this has to do with why we are here on our side of

34

the bridge. We are not here to see the future, but to experience the present. This is how we explore and come to understand ourselves. Surprise is crucial or we will not act out of our deepest truth. We won't get to discover ourselves. So there will always be a limit not only on how much our dead know of the future, but also on how much we can be told.

I would say that my relationship with Anne is deeper now than it was when we were both in the physical. I was her companion in life. Now I am in communion with her. We are, in other words, sharing our beings in ways that are not possible when both are limited by the barrier of the physical. We share our beings and at the same time cultivate questions that will help us both continue the process of discovery that is the core aim of any relationship, including—and especially—one that crosses the bridge.

Teacher that she is, Anne loves the question and understands its value deeply. It would be wonderful to be able to have certainty. But as much as we would rather enjoy the comfort of belief, to live in the adventure of the question is richer, better and, frankly, a great deal more fun.

To our deepest cores and in every drop of our blood we human beings fear to die. It is this crushing fear that can strip the humanity right out of us and turn us violent.

Anne is part of the effort to change this by helping us, the living, to replace the fear that rules us with another approach entirely. It is not a rigid belief, but rather a supple, questioning sense of assurance that this universe isn't simply a passive reality that happens to contain us, but a living presence of which we are a part.

The bright materialism of modern life makes it hard to believe that there is anything more than the body, even though some of us still embrace religious beliefs that tell a different story. But Anne, like my other near-death experiencers who weren't religious, didn't follow the old rituals but did believe in the soul.

She didn't just believe in a subjective sense. Because of her NDE, she felt that she had objective proof of the existence of her soul.

She wrote eloquently about the NDE in Anne's Diary, which she kept on our website, Unknowcountry.com. The entry is called "The Love that Led Me Home" These lines from it are relevant to this discussion: "All that really survives of us is the love we have made in the world. It's a simple truth that will stay with me forever, even when I pass again across the threshold, this time never to return. Especially then."

Anne meant, of course, objective love, the great creative force that binds the world together.

Recently she expanded on the idea when she said to me, "love is the basis of being." In other words, it is something like gravity, without which the material world would not exist. But without love, nothing, not even gravity, would exist. So it isn't just an emotion, but also the fundamental building block of the universe.

That sort of love is what remains of her. It is what our dead are. The love that filled her being has now become her being. This is not to say that she has ceased to exist as a separate person. Far from it.

Her life was and is about creating, teaching and, above all, spreading the energy we know as joy. A few days after she died, one reader of our website wrote, "Anne was strong on my mind during yesterday's commute. I struggled to focus on her message to have joy, instead of crying. Just then a car pulled in front of me. The plate read, 'Joy to U.'"

To me, this was a familiar method of Anne's. About six weeks after she died, I was driving home from a concert on a Saturday afternoon. It was the first time I'd been back to the lovely home where this intimate concert series is held. Anne and I had spent many pleasurable afternoons there, and going back without her had been hard.

Afterward, I was driving along home quietly crying when I heard the a-capella singing group Cantus on Prairie Home Companion. They sang a song called "Wanting Memories."

"I am sitting here wanting memories to teach me, to see the beauty in the world through my own eyes."

"You used to rock me in the cradle of your arms, you said you'd hold me till the pains of life were gone. You said you'd comfort me in times like these and now I need you, now I need you, and you are gone."

"I thought that you were gone, but now I know you're with me, you are the voice that whispers all I need to hear. I know a please a thank you and a smile will take me far, I know that I am you and you are me and we are one, I know that who I am is numbered in each grain of sand, I know that I've been blessed again, and over again."

It was so precisely what I needed to hear that I called her aloud, "Anne, is this from you?" At that moment, I noticed the car in front of me. Its license plate read, "Believe." She was not asking for the empty belief that shuts out the richness of question, but real belief based on the fact that the event was too improbable to be a coincidence.

My teacher, the mistress of the question, was now asking me to believe something, which was that she was definitely with me. From long experience with her, I knew that, once I had accepted this new evidence, fresh questions would follow.

I asked her what they might be and at once found myself thinking about the mission, the building of the bridge. I saw, suddenly, that she might well have lived and died, and left this world when she did, on its behalf.

We do not know our souls' reasons for our lives. We act from hidden direction, and Anne was no exception to this rule. I doubt that she is the only soul with this mission. Indeed, far from it. I sense a whole vast chorus calling to us from the other reality, saying 'awaken, awaken, the time is now.'

But why? Why not fifty years ago or a thousand from now?

There are three reasons: the first is that we must enlist both sides of the "brain" of mankind—the living on the left and what we call the dead on the right—in order, in a very practical way, to thread our way through the upheavals that are coming; the second is that it is possible now and it has not been before. The third reason—dare I say it—is that it's wonderful, joyous fun.

The reason it can happen now is the explosion of near death experiences. Before the medical breakthroughs of the past half century, they were relatively rare. No longer.

Anne was a beneficiary of such medical advances. She had, ten years before her tumor appeared, experienced another extremely dangerous illness. Over its perilous course, she had traveled deep into death. But then the impossible happened: she returned. Medical advances that had only taken place in the previous few years enabled her improbable survival.

She had ventured deep into the undiscovered country, returning as a modern version of the shaman, a master of travel between the worlds. And she had a message: that country is undiscovered no longer. We come and go, and we are learning the secrets of this greatest of all journeys. Our modern shamen—walkers between the worlds—are the growing legion of people like Anne, the near-death experiencers.

This is their revolution, both those on this side of the bridge and those on the other.

CHAPTER 4

"Whitley, I Need Your Help"

OUR WORLD EXPLODED in our faces for the first time on a rainy Saturday in October of 2004. We were in Los Angeles working and visiting our kids. We'd had lunch, then gone to a movie. Then we went to our son's house and watched a baseball game with him and his girlfriend.

A peaceful, normal day. Two people long-ago grown together, deeply in love.

All was well.

The minutes of the day passed without remark, time slipping away as it usually does in the sweetness of life. We knew nothing of what was happening inside Anne's brain, a tiny vein bulging more and more. The defect had probably been there since birth, causing no symptoms and never noticed.

A year before, she had begun suffering from a nerve inflammation in her buttocks called periformis syndrome. It had come from playing racquetball too hard and sitting on a badly constructed couch. She'd been taking Aleve for it—too much Aleve for a person with a brain defect like the one she had. But nobody knew.

As we watched the Yankees and the Red Sox, the crisis silently approached, a ticking bomb, ticking faster and faster. Unheard.

After the game, we got in our car and drove to our temporary rental apartment—coincidentally on Whitley Terrace in the Hollywood Hills. In the car we spoke quietly about the coming evening. I was due to go on Art Bell's Coast-to-Coast radio show in about an hour, and as always Anne would be at my side, listening, feeding me ideas, doing everything she could to support me. She would come on the show as well.

On the way, she said, "I want you to know I've had a wonderful marriage."

She sounded grave and introspective. I replied, "Oh, honey, me too!"

I wondered why she'd said it, such a serious thing at what seemed to be an entirely trivial, commonplace moment.

Tick, tick, tick.

There was not the slightest sign that her life might end before the clock struck nine. It was eight forty.

She was now very quiet. What she wasn't saying was that she had a terrific headache and it was building fast. Anne did not report symptoms. As a girl, when she had done so, she had been accused of trying to avoid her chores. All through our marriage I had tried to get her to change this deeply ingrained habit, but without success.

When we reached the apartment, she had literally only minutes to live. By now, her head must have been pounding. The moment I stopped, she jumped out of the car and went racing into the flat.

A little surprised but not yet concerned, I followed her.

As I walked in, I heard her call from the bathroom, "Whitley, I need your help."

I could see her standing with an open bottle of Aleve in her hands. Her eyes rolled back into her head and her legs buckled. I caught her on the way down and, protecting her head, got her to the floor.

At that moment the phone rang. It was Art Bell. I shouted to him that Anne had collapsed and hung up. Then I called 911 and then my son, who started over immediately.

I went back to Anne, made sure she had a good airway and was still breathing.

It was obvious that she was in terrible distress. I didn't know what was wrong, but this looked to me like a person who was dying, and quickly. Her lips were slack, her eyes rolled back in her head, her pulse racing, her breathing becoming erratic.

I began CPR. Our son arrived, then had to go chasing off down the street after the EMS wagon, which couldn't find the address. But then they were there, oxygenating her and setting her up to travel.

Maybe ten minutes left, maybe less.

In total shock, my son and I followed the wagon to a nearby hospital. I told him to prepare himself. My heart was thundering, I was being rocked to the core of my being by the absolute suddenness of the change. No warning, no idea at all that anything was wrong.

I thought that she might well be dead by the time we got to the emergency room, but as we walked in, I could see her being wheeled into a cubicle, clearly still alive.

When the doctor came out to see us, he was frank. She'd had a hemorrhagic stroke—a brain bleed—and it was a bad one. Her prognosis was, as he put it, "very guarded."

While we waited, I looked up the statistics and saw that she had only a small chance of survival. Then I saw that if she did, she might well end up severely impaired.

Another blow: our life together was probably over, and if not, then it was likely to get much harder. The remarkable, beautiful, immeasurably alive woman I loved might well be gone forever, or left in ruins.

Thus began the greatest battle of both of our lives. While Anne fought to survive, I fought to make certain that everything was done for her that could be done, and that it was done right.

Little did I know that Anne was already dead. She was no longer in her body, but rather was taking a journey that in the past used to be a final one. She had become an explorer in the undiscovered country.

She found herself in what she later described as sort of way station, like a railroad terminal or a subway stop. It was filled with people sitting on benches, clutching bags and suitcases. It was clear that nobody was leaving that station, not while they clung to their burdens. Then Anne heard a voice say to her, "you can go on, or you can go back if you wish."

She had no burdens in her hands. She wasn't clinging to anything. But she did have a husband she loved and a son in his twenties who had not yet started his family.

Our Persephone, our underworld journeyer, had a decision to make. Would she return to her family, or travel on into the bright realm she could see ahead?

As I have said, Anne was a teacher to her core. It was and is the essential reality of her soul, her truth. She also had a life goal that was deeply important to her, which was to create a family that was better and stronger than what either of us had known.

She had raised a wonderful son. He had found a fine young woman. She had a family to nurture.

Maybe somebody on the other side thought she could come back, but what was happening on this side was that we were losing her. The hospital to which she'd first been taken— the closest one—was not equipped to deal with a brain bleed as bad as hers. The most they could do was to temporarily stop it.

We had to take her, loaded with stents and tubes, on a dangerous journey across town to the UCLA Medical Center. I rode with her in the ambulance, my heart almost stopping with every jostle and every bump. But she made it and was soon in an intensive care unit that specialized in strokes. Half the patients in it were bleed victims, and hardly a day passed when one of them wasn't quietly removed to the hospital's basement morgue.

When Anne was in intensive care, I lived in the hall. Time and again, the staff gently threw me out, but I would wait until the coast was clear and then go back to my perch beside the door. Family members were not allowed in the ICU except at certain hours, and sometimes not even then. It depended on how busy the nurses were.

So unless you were there when the door opened, you might not see your patient for hours. I knew that Anne wanted me beside her. I could feel it very clearly and strongly. Sometimes, I could see her in the hall, standing before me, looking down at me gravely and curiously.

In normal life, there was an aura around Anne. Her eyes were bright with intelligence, her mind was quick, she was extremely well informed, she was witty. But there was more— that glow.

When Anne first came to me, this light—unlike any I had ever known—had entered my life. Compared to her, the girls I had known before were sweet shadows.

Now here was this bright being brought low. To me, it seemed as if nature had committed a sin against itself. She belonged to sunlight and happy days, not to this cruel struggle.

When I was allowed into the ICU, she would look at me with searching eyes. Because of her intubation, she could not speak.

I sat beside her bed praying the Hail Mary and the Lord's Prayer from my Catholic childhood. When I was in my car, I prayed the repetitive Jesus Prayer, "Lord Jesus Christ have mercy on me," but I changed the words to "on her." I went to sleep praying and woke up praying, and when I wasn't praying I went deep into the sensing exercise I had been doing since we joined the Gurdjieff Work in 1970, passing my attention from one limb to the next, until I was everywhere in my flesh, not just riding the mind. Over the years, I had found that sensation deepened, slowly becoming something more than just awareness of the body. The exercise is simple, but also an amazingly effective way of opening the inner door to the soul. This is because in life soul and body are so intermingled that it is very hard to tell the difference. When by chance the attention extends into the soul level, there may be a startling moment of awakening. The world seems then quite new, quite unexpected, even magical. But there was little magic for me then.

Normally, soul and body in concert sailed the fears of those nights. They still do, but no longer in fear. I am like a companionship within myself now, the ego and the physical appetites directing the body to act, the body acting, and the soul watching, my dear friend who is also me, and more of me than I am.

But then—those days—I was so afraid that Anne would miss seeing her family grow. Selfishly speaking, I could not imagine life without her. I had to save my wife!

When I was too tired to go on and had to sleep, I would comfort myself by holding one of her nightgowns close to me. The black dogs of fear would run in my mind. Again and again I would ask myself how I could live without her. I did not know. I could not imagine. And her life was so unfinished! The kids had to get married, there had to be grandchildren, and she had to see that! I knew somehow deep in myself that this had to be. When she left this world, she had to be free. Nothing essential must be left undone.

But even as we struggled to keep her alive, she went deeper and deeper into the world of the dead.

As the doctors pumped fluids into her body to combat the brain swelling, she blew up like a balloon. It was done to keep the tiny inter-cranial capillaries open. Wherever that blood flow failed, that part of her brain would die.

Then another crisis: the fluid load was causing her blood pressure to rise astronomically. But the treatment had to be continued as long as there was blood in her spinal fluid and her brain was swollen.

Her blood pressure rose—150, 180, 210, then higher and higher yet. The treatment that was keeping her brain from being destroyed was now raising the specter of stroke.

An agonizing decision was laid before me. Should they continue treatment and take the risk of a catastrophic stroke, or should they stop and risk a degree of impairment? No matter which they did, death would always be a possibility.

Death, death everywhere! It was surrounding us like a thick, black fog.

If I decided to stop the therapy and she came out disabled, how would she feel about her life then? About me?

Again and again, I read her living will, written carefully

in her own hand. No resuscitation if no hope of survival. Everything possible to be done prior to that.

But what about impairment? She said nothing about it.

I went to the hospital's chapel and prayed more. I went to mass and afterward tried to get counseling from the priest, but I cried so much I couldn't express myself.

The doctors were waiting. They needed a decision. I asked my son what he thought.

"Dad, mom would not like to be in a wheelchair.." No, but who would? She'd get used to it, people do.

Then I thought, 'what if she lost her ability to think clearly?'

That decided it. Anne would prefer death to that.

I could almost feel her next to me as I went to tell the doctor on the unit that Triple H therapy was to be continued until her spinal fluid was clear.

So we waited, watching the blood pressure monitor, watching the shunt that circulated her spinal fluid, waiting for that faint pinkness to clear.

Day after agonizing day, we prayed and watched and waited. Then, one day, I was told that her fluid was clear and the therapy could be stopped.

But was she damaged? Could they tell?

A few days later she came awake—and she seemed fine!

She knew me, she knew herself, our son, remembered her life, all of it. A therapy dog came to visit and she petted it. She spoke normally with me. The doctors talked of a release.

To say that I was elated would be an understatement. For the first time in weeks, I slept a good sleep. We were home free, we had made it through one of the most dangerous illnesses known to man.

But then, the next morning, she wouldn't wake up. Worse, her temperature was rising. At noon she was diagnosed with spinal meningitis.

By this time I'd read a great deal about Anne's disease and I knew of this danger. I knew that death had returned.

She was administered broad spectrum antibiotics, but her fever rose and rose. The doctors were having difficulty identifying the bacillus that was causing the infection. The antibiotics were useless.

In even the recent past, this latest catastrophe would have been her last, and it is during this time that I believe she was having her near-death experience. Then they identified the bacillus. A new antibiotic therapy was begun. But she was so full of infection that even though the right antibiotic had been found, it was still touch-and-go. Her temperature continued to rise.

If it could not be brought down, she was going to either die or suffer yet another form of brain damage.

The nurses had gotten used to my constant presence and were making use of me as a volunteer. I watched over her every moment, day and night, sleeping only in fits and starts. When the ICU had to be cleared, they simply closed the curtains around us.

By this time in our life together, I was well aware that my wife was a spiritual expert. I had seen the grace and ease with which she taught others, always without them realizing it, drawing them to moments of richly revealing inlooking. She did this with me all the time, always with love and skill and her wonderful humor.

Only a master can do that because only a master can see the truth of souls.

I was not going to lose this woman. I was not going to see her value lost when she was still in the prime of life.

But if that particular ambition was to be fulfilled, her temperature had to come down, and soon.

My son and I spent all one night keeping her body cool with wet towels. The danger was in the wee hours, the time when defenses are at their weakest. We applied towels, the antibiotics dripped and her temperature continued to rise.

It went on and on like that, hour after hour. The nurses spelled us but they also used us as volunteers for which we were both grateful. We didn't want to be away from her for a single instant.

It became hypnotic, soaking the towels in the ice buckets the nurses were bringing, applying them until they were warm, then doing it again. Through it all she slept the sleep of eternity.

Then, at about four in the morning I noticed that the readout had dropped a tenth of a point. But it went back up so quickly that I thought I had hallucinated.

The nurses began watching her closely, two of them now helping us keep her cool. Her temperature dropped a tenth of a degree, then another tenth. Another. By five thirty, the tension of struggle had left her face. She was sleeping peacefully. Her temperature was 98.9 and still dropping.

As dawn slipped in, we slumped exhausted into the chairs beside the bed. Later, when she had been normal for a few hours, we drove back to the apartment for showers and sleep. We both sensed that another miracle had occurred. The nurses and doctors had clearly not expected what had happened.

A few days later, she was so improved that it was possible to remove her tubes. Except for those few lucid hours now three weeks ago, I had not been able to speak with her since before her bleed. I would be able to talk to her, to find out what she had been experiencing through all of this.

But when she could speak, it turned out that she had acquired something known as "ICU psychosis."

My brilliant wife with her razor-sharp mind was completely off her head.

She was moved to the transitional intensive care unit. On the doctor's instruction, I talked to her endlessly, working to bring her back to the real world. Hour after hour she babbled on. Hour after hour I told her that her fantasies were wrong. Our son came and helped me. We spelled each other. As I recall, she talked continuously for something like fifty hours. When she finally fell asleep, so did we!

Finally, it came time to release her from the ICU area into the general population. Once she was settled in, I left her alone for the first night in a long time. But she became completely uncontrollable. She did not know where she was and she was terrified. She kept leaving the room, calling for our doctor in Texas, a lifelong friend. But we were in California. The nurses had no idea who he was.

I was called and I rushed back to the hospital. When she saw me she ran up to me and threw her arms around me. "Oh, thank God, thank God! I thought you'd left me! I thought I was alone!"

"I'll be beside you every second from now on."

That night, I slept on my side on her narrow bed, and the next night and the next. Finally, they gave me a chaise lounge and I slept in it. I never let go of her hand, and again and again in the night, she would whisper, "Whitty?" and I would say, "I'm here."

One day, given her continued improvement and the need for beds, the resident decided to discharge her.

I was appalled. I told him that it was too soon. During an illness like hers, debris builds up in the areas of the brain where spinal fluid circulates. This material can clog the tiny passages that allow the flow to continue. If that happens, fluid builds up in the brain. If left untreated, this hydrocephalus becomes dangerous, even catastrophic.

He reacted to me with arrogance and open contempt that some stupid caregiver would dare to question him. The next thing I knew she was no longer an inpatient. I tried to protest to the head of neuro-surgery but he could not be reached.

She was sent to rehabilitation. But they would not allow her into the hospital's rehab unit because it had a door that led directly to the street and they were afraid she'd blunder out. So she was transferred to another hospital, which proved to be something out of a Dickens novel. I was regarded by everyone I encountered with beady-eyed contempt and wariness. Apparently my reputation as a 'hands on' caregiver had preceded me.

Fifteen minutes after she was admitted, she fell asleep. It was noon and she'd slept all night. But the move had been tiring, I thought. I sat beside her, waiting for her to wake up.

She did not wake up. Finally, in the evening, I tried to rouse her but she remained asleep. In fact, she was not asleep, she was uncon-scious. I told the nurses about this, but was ignored. I went back to my son's place but neither of us could sleep and at two in the morning we returned to the hospital.

I examined her, lifting her eyelids, feeling her pulse, trying to rouse her.

She was nearly in a coma.

I immediately went to the nurses' station and reported that Anne had hydrocephalus and needed to get to an emergency room immediately. (This rehab hospital didn't have one.)

The nurses laughed in my face and told me to go home. I knew that I had only so much time to save her. But at least this time it was hours, not minutes.

In the morning, I called our doctor in Texas. He managed to get the number of the hospital's on-call neurologist. The nurses had refused to call her or to give me the number.

At length, I got her on the phone. She came in and confirmed that Anne was hydrocephalic. I immediately telephoned the head of neurosurgery at UCLA and told him that she needed to be readmitted. The neurologist talked to him and concurred. But then another glitch: the hospital refused to take her back!

This had all taken until three in the afternoon and I was now frantic. Anne was close to a coma. I told the nursing staff that I wanted all of their names because I was going to sue not only the hospital, but each of them personally. The next thing I knew, a guard was lurking nearby.

Finally, I telephoned my brother, who is a lawyer, and he called the head of UCLA neurosurgery and said to him that the premature release was a clear case of malpractice and if Anne wasn't back in the hospital in an hour, he could expect a suit to be filed forthwith.

Twenty minutes later, an ambulance showed up and we were on our way back to UCLA. A surgery was performed to install a shunt under her scalp that would enable her spinal fluid to circulate again. This was successful and she spent some more time in the ICU, then once again entered the general population.

She had wandered far during her various crises, going deep into an unknown world of incoherence, confusion and, eventually, a sort of poetry. But now, finally, when the pressure was relieved, she was coherent.

She said, "My last memory is of you dancing around like a vaudeville performer."

"Yeah," I said, "I've been doing a bit of dancing."

We were finally in the UCLA rehab unit. She had been admitted on the understanding that I would live in the unit with her and never leave her side. That was fine by me. In fact, I was delighted. Right next to her was exactly where I wanted to be.

As she gradually regained more and more coherence, she suddenly announced, "Coe! Coe is here."

Persephone had returned from the underworld and those four simple words were her first message from the beyond, the first suggestion that she'd had a near-death experience.

Our little Siamese cat, named Coe by our son at the age of six, had died five years previously. I thought that Anne might have been dreaming, but also that it was possible that she had seen him during an NDE. Pets are sometimes encountered.

Over the next few days, she began to talk more about where she'd been and what she'd seen. I listened without questioning her, letting her proceed at her own pace. But I was pretty sure by now that I had indeed had an NDE.

The fact that she had lived to describe her journey is the foundational reality of the afterlife revolution. Medical science had defied death and saved her, and in so doing enabled yet another near-death experiencer to bring her story back rather than disappearing with it into the unknown.

These new pathfinders like Anne and so many others are our best chance—and first real chance—to find our way out of the hell of fear and cruelty that is our world and into the wholeness of a truly mature species, where the physical and nonphysical sides work together.

Anne had been transformed. She had a completely new vision of reality. Her mission remained unstated as such, but she had been put on its path by the breathtaking power of her NDE. Again and again, she would tell the story of it, always concluding with that statement, "we have to put those burdens down or we're not going anywhere."

This modern shaman, like so many others, had been initiated not by death-tempting rites but by death-defying medical procedures.

It used to be a rare thing for a person to actually complete an initiation. The ancient rituals were generally dangerous, often very much so. But that was the point. They were about tempting death.

The ones who had entered the world of the dead and been resurrected were considered remarkable and indeed, they were very rare. The stories they brought back remain to this day at the center of much human religious belief and practice. Books like the Tibetan Book of the Dead and the Egyptian Pyramid Texts are based on observations from such journeys. But they are not ideal texts for our era. The journeys they chronicle are described in terms of mythology that could be understood by the people of the eras in which they were written, but which do not resonate with us now, not in our secular and de-mythologized culture.

Most of the new near death travelers come to their experiences, as Anne did, with essentially no preconceptions about what this other reality might be like and what they might expect to see.

There are consistencies, though. An experience of entering an encompassing and loving light is often described—the literal manifestation of Anne's 'objective love.' The approach of dead friends and relatives is very commonly reported. Journeys into worlds that seem to be almost physically real also appear frequently in the considerable literature that has emerged as the field of near-death studies.

Near-death experiencers are the wonder workers of modern times, leading us into an entirely new understanding of and relationship with our own souls. They challenge us to revisit our entire approach to death and dying. Their reports suggest that the soul is not only real, but that what we think of as reality is actually a small corner of a much larger world. They suggest that consciousness is not only in us and part of us, but more that we are in consciousness, journeying through a world largely unseen by us in bodies that appear to be designed to filter out any vision of the larger reality.

When Anne was alive, her relationship to the divine was private but powerful. I feel that she was closer to God than anyone else I have ever known. She would say, "We don't know what god is," but also, "God is my best friend."

Many an NDE experiencer would agree, I think. God seems to be a living mystery to them, at once a familiar friend and an unknowable presence.

This is a much different vision of deity than we are used to. This combining of the comfortably familiar and the completely mysterious points the way to nothing less than a new understanding of man, universe and the sacred that both acknowledges the reality and accepts the mystery.

I cannot ever fully express how completely my wife's NDE changed her. She was so unafraid of death that it was, frankly, astonishing. She laughed at it. She was always happy, full of the joy of spirit that comes with the relief of great fear.

Our teachers—the near-death experiencers—are pointing the way to this new way of being human and this new kind of mankind—free of belief, past all the confusions of mythology, and yet more spiritually alive than ever before.

The awe that has distanced us from heaven for so many generations is imploding. Their god—Anne's god—isn't on any sort of a throne. Far from it. This new god is so much like us that he she and it might be us.

Man in god. Man as god.

Anne would say these things and she would laugh and I would laugh too, and I would wonder, 'what has my wife become?'

She had become herself, truly, a human being in full wakefulness, spreading her message as best she could in a sleeping world.

CHAPTER 5

Laughter and Shadows

ANNE MIGHT NEVER HAVE CALLED herself a teacher, but I had recognized early on what she had to offer, and I was certainly using her as one. As to being a master, she scorned that sort of label. "Anybody who calls themselves a master isn't one and when a real master is called that, he laughs."

Laughter. She would often repeat a quote of Anne Lamott's, "If you want to make god laugh, tell her your plans." She used to say, "You know what the word in John was, the logos? Laughter. That was the word of power that started it all." The Gospel of John begins with the sentence, "In the beginning was the word and the word was with God, and the word was God."

If you asked her if she knew god, she would laugh, but that laughter had something in it that was great with wisdom.

She would say, "that's a crazy question." Then she'd look at me and her eyes would say, "no it's not."

I could have conversations with her like this: Me: "Who is god?"

Anne: "We are."

Me: "Then who are we?"

She would smile, looking inward, and say no more.

A form of meditation called the sensing exercise centers my spiritual life. To do it, you sit quietly and place your attention on your body, first one limb and then another, then your torso and head, until you are no longer in your mind, but concentrating your attention on your body.

Anne did not do it much, neither before nor after her NDE. This is because to her everything was always new, all the time. She used to say that she noticed everything, and this was quite true. Although on the surface she seemed an entirely normal person, there was also within my wife the powerful, loving stillness I had seen when I first met her. It was this stillness—this part of her—that saw so much.

She had always been tolerant of the posturing and egotism of others—including this one. After her NDE, this changed. She became much more urgent. Previously, she'd hoped you would see. Now she couldn't contain herself. You had to see that you had a soul and that it mattered terribly.

She would lead you into an instance of self-revelation that could be devastating. Then she'd say sweetly, "Oh, dear, did I say the wrong thing?"

Hardly.

She did not suffer fools, and the temper of the early years became a tool she used to draw people into seeing themselves. She was the fiercest gentle person I ever knew.

She had understood identification from our years in the Work but after the NDE she was really focused on it. I'm not sure that she was consciously aware of this, but I learned a long time ago not to question my wife's level of awareness about anything. I don't know what she did out of deep, unconscious knowledge and what was done from conscious awareness.

I do know, however, why a person with awareness of the needs of the soul and the consequences of living in ego, would be so intent on helping people learn to use their personalities as tools of their souls rather than letting their personalities use them.

I was sitting reading one afternoon when a celebrity who had died the day before appeared in my mind's eye. He said, "What am I supposed to do now?"

I didn't know him personally at all. I knew his work, of course, some of which had been quite good. I knew that he had been involved in charitable work, also.

He was wandering in this level of reality, and I knew from experience that this was because he couldn't see any other place to go. For souls in that state, the physical world is as enclosing as it is for us. What you have to do is turn them around. It's hard. It often doesn't work. But when such people show up, I always try.

I said that there was a light behind him. I could see it there, though it was very dim. He said, "Who are you?" I told him my name and he replied, "You're some nobody. I expected to be met by Mother Theresa or somebody like that."

I laughed and replied, "She's not here."

He went away and I lost contact with him for a time. When I saw him again, he had realized that he had been extremely cruel in his life and was literally twisted with regret.

He will wander in this level maybe for a long time, slowly shedding his big ego and the bad memories that go with it. Once he is just a tiny fragment, he'll probably drift into a womb and return to this world, more or less at random.

Anne didn't want anybody to suffer that. In fact, she didn't want anybody to suffer at all. Thus her willingness to infuriate people in the interest of helping them see their arrogance and hopefully escape it.

Much of my inner work with the visitors has from the beginning involved gaining control over ego, and Anne came back from her NDE with a master's ability to work with it.

Even before that, she'd been aware of how it can get in the way of inner growth, and was always eager to challenge it. She had seen how the visitors worked to help me get mine under control.

Once I was making a speech before a large audience. She sat in the front row. Normally, she would listen to every word and afterward, her eyes filled with admiration, compliment me on how well I had done. But this time, just as I started to speak, she stood up and walked out on me. She went marching off down the aisle with every eye on her.

I was appalled. But what could I do? I had to give my speech. As I did so, I saw my ego with more clarity than I ever had before in my life. Standing on that podium, I also found myself standing outside of my own personality, watching it as it postured and performed for the audience.

Afterward, I asked her why she'd done what she did. She said, "Oh, I'd heard it all before." Then her eyes met mine with such frankness, such love and such deep humor that all I could do was thank her.

I asked her, "How did it feel to walk out like that?" She laughed.

If she saw in you a weakness that was undermining your soul's health, she was going to try to help you. She wanted us to see with new eyes, and true eyes. That was her goal, often stated.

One would be bragging away, lost in self-regard, when she would make some small, seemingly offhand comment, or just glance at you in a certain way, that would make you realize that you were completely full of yourself. In an instant, she could set you on a new and better path, one that was oriented toward living a more loving and selfless life, and a more humble one. And your vision would expand.

The understanding of God that she'd brought back with her was at once subtle and simple—and yet also light and full of fun.

A particularly important example of what I mean took place in 2012—it was, in fact, the first of the "license plate communications" that would later happen to me and others after her death.

I was in meditation one afternoon when I saw in my mind's eye a dog I had known in my youth. He was called Quagmire because he was always a mess. His was a troubled family and he lived a hard life. But he was always happy. No matter how difficult things were for him, you could always count on Quag to bring a sloppy lick of joy up to your face.

I had not thought of this dog at all since I was a teenager.

When I told Anne about it, she said, "Dog-God. You just had a visit from God."

God? Was she kidding? God was a distant, immeasurable and awe-inspiring presence. I said, "I'd need some sort of a sign if I was going to believe that."

Half an hour later we left on our afternoon walk. And there, parked at the curb in front of our house was a car with the vanity plate QGMIRE. Quagmire. A coincidence, but also too much of one. She said something along the lines of, "He's ready to be your dog even though it's his universe. So lighten up and let it happen."

I thought about all the lessons I had received from the visitors about humility, and decided to just accept what had happened, and let Anne be my guide.

My totem animal, as a shaman might call Quag, became the dog—in fact, this particular dog, shaggy, ordinary and joyous even in his suffering.

In our many future conversations about the sacred, Anne always referred not to god but to dog. "Dog's going to be disappointed, Whitley, if you do such and such." Or, "Ask Dog. Dog will help you."

Dog did, and does. Dog's here and he's not going anywhere. But then again, how can he? He's everywhere. I cannot count the number of times since that day that dogs have showed up in my mind's eye while meditating, or in my dreams or my life.

In childhood, I had a pet dog called Candy, a little rat terrier. We were inseparable. When, during Anne's first visit to my childhood home, she peeked in on me while I was sleeping, she saw Candy's head on the pillow beside mine. Afterward, she would often laugh and say, "I discovered that I had a rival!"

Sometime in 2008, I was asleep beside Anne in bed and found myself stroking Candy just as I had when I was a boy. I thought to myself, 'I wonder how old Candy is now?' We'd gotten her in 1953 when I was eight, so—I calculated in my head—and I sat straight up in bed. Candy would be nearly sixty.

Then I realized that it was just a very vivid dream.

Next morning, Anne said, "It wasn't a dream." Then she laughed. "She's back, darn it!"

Some weeks later, Candy appeared again. This time, she brought a strange vision with her. It was of a dark, narrow road bordered on both sides by bushes. Anne and I are riding in a car. Ahead in the distance, the lights of another vehicle appear. I think to myself, 'if we don't turn around right now, we'll die on this road.'

Anne was a skilled interpreter of dreams. She always had been, since long before her NDE. "That was a warning, Whitley. If you're ever on a road like that, turn around."

A few months later we were in England at a conference in the town of Devises. A friend invited us to visit Stonehenge for a special evening tour, so we rented a car. Driving on the left was always a struggle for me, but I seemed to be managing. Soon we were on a narrow road bordered by bushes. It was nearly dark.

Anne said, "Whitley?"

"I'm okay," I snapped. But I was hardly that. I could barely keep the car on the road.

Ahead of us lights appeared, just as in the "dream." "Turn around now," Anne said quietly.

The lights raced toward us.

I realized that I didn't have mine on. As I fumbled to find the switch, the car came closer and closer. I pulled onto the verge, smashing into the shrubs.

The car raced past us. I doubt if the driver ever saw us. Anne said, "Candy just saved our lives."

I took the car straight back to the rental station. We never went to Stonehenge.

As I look back, I find that my life before Anne was that of a wanderer. I had been lost in a kind of labyrinth. I wanted to be a writer, but I didn't know how to do it. But then, in the spring of 1969, there she was, this time as Ariadne with her thread in hand, ready to guide me out of my confusion.

Our powerful mutual attraction caused us to decide to combine our meager resources. We weren't married and couldn't afford to get married. We had to first save up that two hundred dollars, and with my salary of $125 a week and rent of $125 a month and the fact that she kept getting fired, that took a while.

She was living in a miserable little room in Queens, me in a tiny apartment in Manhattan. But it was at least in Manhattan, so she moved in with me. The place was a shambles, furnished with a seedy couch and a bed loaned to me by the superintendent of the building. When Anne first came in, she took a look around and said, "It has possibilities," and she didn't only mean the apartment.

She arrived with a single small suitcase and a cardboard box, which together contained all her belongings. It took us ten minutes to move her in and we started our life together.

We didn't have money for books but both loved to read. So we pooled our money and shared them. We also started library member-ships. At first, she just read mysteries. But when she discovered that I wanted to be a writer and was working on a novel in the evenings after coming home from my advertising job, she turned to more serious fiction.

My ambition at once became a major focus of Anne's life. She read every page I wrote, and proved to be an insightful editor and a wonderful source of ideas. It seemed natural for her to be a muse. She was marvelous at it.

Nevertheless, I got rejection after rejection. In fact, my first readers who were members of the public came to me because of a rejection. I'd sent a novel to an agent, who had responded that she'd like to see more of my work. So I sent her my latest opus, a book called Catherine's Bounty. For weeks, I heard nothing. Then one Saturday morning there was a knock at the door. It was an off-duty postman. He had my manuscript tied up in a neat bundle. He said that he'd found it in the bottom of a mailbox with no postage on it, not even an envelope around it, just a heap of pages. The agent had simply tossed it in, as if into the garbage. As the postman gathered it up, he found my name and address on the title page. He said, "It's really good. My wife and I both read it and we loved it."

Anne not only completed her BA, she got a masters in education from the prestigious Bank Street College of Education and taught grade school for some years. She did it in an entirely unique way, getting with her kids on a one-to-one basis, coming to them on their own terms. And they loved her for it. She helped them fill their school hallways with murals. In our neighborhood she was known as "the paint lady" because she strolled around covered with paint. She thought nothing of things like that. She wasn't afraid to simply be herself. It never occurred to her to live in any other way.

As the years went on, I came to understand and appreciate her ways more and more. She lived out of herself as she was. She contrived nothing, she concealed nothing. When you knew my wife, you knew her truth.

Over time, our love deepened more and more. One without the other came to seem inconceivable.

This happy life was disrupted and complicated by the Communion experience and its aftermath, but the happiness of just being together remained the currency of our relationship. Our friends used to joke that we were more like a single person with two bodies than a couple.

We lived in love, in the false eternity of the years. We were poor, we were rich, we were poor again. Our son grew up and thrived. No matter what happened in our lives, at the end of the day we could lie in one another's arms in the sweet dark.

And then there came, seemingly out of nowhere, the last shadow. Until the moment it happened, we had not the slightest idea that a final night was falling on our life.

By 2013, Anne was completely recovered from her stroke. Her illness was long in the past. It was easy to forget that it had even happened.

But then, in the wee hours of a morning in February of 2013, the terror began again. Anne had been suffering from a heavy cold and had been taking cough medicine at night so she could sleep. One night when she had finally managed to fall asleep, I was awakened by a strange movement in the bed, a sort of steady shuddering.

I turned on the light to find her in a full seizure. It had come completely out of the blue. For a moment, I watched her. I called to her. There was no response. She was blacked out, her eyes rolled back in her head, her mouth working, her whole body trembling.

I at once dialed 911 and EMS was there within minutes. By then the seizure had ended but she was still unconscious. I watched as she was prepared for transport to the hospital. On the way to the ambulance, she came to. She had no idea who she was or who I was. Her entire life appeared to have been erased.

I found myself once again following an ambulance with my beloved in it. Once again, there came a night of agonized waiting.

She was taken into radiology for evaluation. I feared the worst. I thought she had a brain tumor. When she came back, she had pretty much recovered her faculties. She had returned to normal.

I waited, sick with fear, for the MRI report to come back. When it did, I was amazed that it said that her brain was normal. The ER doctor thought perhaps the seizure had been caused by a reaction to the cold medicine.

Even though, once back home, she seemed to return to normal, I still did not believe the report. I wished I could see the actual MRI, but at the time I didn't know how to obtain it from the hospital. Given her history of so many CT scans during her illness, I knew perfectly well that she could have cancer. But there was also another reason that I was concerned about cancer, and in fact, any unusual illness.

Back in the early nineties in our old cabin, I woke up one night to see a purple glow coming from the living room. I hurried along the corridor to see what was going on downstairs and observed a purple ball of light below. It was hanging over the couch. Our older cat, a Burmese called Sadie, was creeping toward it.

I thought, 'if I could get a picture, that would really be something,' and raced back down the corridor to grab the camera that I kept at my bedside. Before I could return, a purple flash filled the house and

61

darkness returned. I went downstairs to find both cats curled up on the floor sound asleep. They could not be roused.

The next morning poor Sadie came crawling along the hallway yowling. We could see purple-pink tumors in both of her eyes. They had appeared overnight. We took her to the vet, who diagnosed cancer. There was no choice but to put our dear old cat lady down.

Many years later I read in a declassified British Ministry of Defense document called the "Condign Report" that there was a type of ionizing radiation associated with "unknown plasmas" that causes trouble for people who are exposed to it.

I think that it's pretty clear that the plasma in the living room is what gave Sadie cancer. So, had it also affected Anne? She had been sleeping at the far end of the house, but there is no way to know. Personally, I think it more likely that she was a victim of too many CT scans during her struggle with the brain bleed. But at least she got ten good years during which she saw her son married and witnessed the birth of both of her grandkids.

I'd had a hard time believing the MRI report, but could not get an early appointment with anyone at UCLA who could take a look at the actual scan. So we went to a neurologist associated with St. John's, another local hospital. I told him I was worried that the report was wrong and I wanted him to look at the MRI. He agreed to do this, but UCLA proved difficult to deal with. They would not release the scan, only the report.

When new seizures took place in April, I didn't call EMS. I had made it my business to learn about the type of seizure she was having and kept her airway clear when they took place.

I lay beside her with my arm around her, knowing that our path had just taken a very dangerous turn. In the morning, I told her of the seizures, but not of the probability that they announced a brain tumor, not yet.

I phoned the neurologist and asked him again to get the scan, to warn UCLA that the patient was once again seizing and he needed that scan at once.

The next morning, I received a truly terrible phone call. It was the neurologist. He had the scan and it showed what he described as an "angry" brain tumor. He told us to get to the UCLA ER at once because they were the only ones nearby with the capability of dealing with such an extensive and aggressive brain cancer.

On the way over, Anne was calm and composed. For my part, I was absolutely terrified. I was losing her. I felt it. My precious lover and dearest friend, my muse, my editor, my teacher, my dear, brilliant angel and the keeper of my heart— how could I hope to save her from an angry brain tumor?

The surgery was scheduled for a few days hence.

Those days of waiting were so sweet, a dark and strangely lovely time in our lives. I cannot express how the minutes felt, each so precious, little jewels falling away forever, one by one.

At night I lay looking at her. I kissed her sleeping face again and again. I hardly slept.

She, by contrast, was completely at peace, and through it all—the surgery, the struggle that followed—that peace never left her.

She died knowing that she had done two brilliant things, one a triumph of the mind, the other one of the heart. Her wonderful, supple mind had understood the close encounter experience and that lovely heart had led to the fulfillment of her ambition to start a family. "I think we're good, Whitley.

I think we should leave as many Striebers in the world as we can."

She did all she could.

She didn't say it at first, but she was ready to go from the beginning. Neither of us wanted this couple to end, but she was accepting of her fate.

I was not. I struggled against it, trying nutrition, cannabis, all sorts of alternative cures. I explored all the different clinical trials, but she wasn't eligible for any of the promising ones.

She accepted my desperate hope that she would survive and took radiotherapy and the anti-cancer drug Temodar. She went on a cannabis regimen that included a daily dose of cannabidiol, or CBD.

The result of all this was that the tumor stopped. But then, about a year into our struggle, the strokes started, and once again she approached the threshold of life.

Her passing was the most fearless and noble human act that I personally have ever witnessed. Every moment of every one of her last days—of all her days—is engraved on my heart as an inspiration to approach my own death in such peace and with such courage.

I sensed when she left that a great soul had ascended. You could feel it in the room, in the very air, a beautiful and fine event—not only a tragedy but also a triumph of nature.

She says, "Don't forget to say that what looks like death to you looks like birth to us. The same second that you lost me, I found a new world."

Now two years after her passing, as I write I look up to a photograph of her. I am still her husband and not just in memory and dream. We are not the only married couple for whom "till death do us part" has ceased to have meaning. Very quietly, hidden away from the scorn and disbelief of the people who cling to the old, dying reality, a new one is being born, and rich, fulfilling relationships between the living and what we call the dead are at the center of it.

People like Anne are forging this new mankind. It is coming out of a more clear understanding of what life and death really are. Our scientists and intellectuals, for the most part committed to the old secular ideology and the cultural empowerment it affords them, disdain the very idea that the dead may persist.

Anne says, "We're not dead. That must be somebody else." They are going to bring their revolution anyway, no matter what we are told to believe by the priests of mind and laboratory. They will not be stopped because what they are bringing is true, and they know it, and we need it and our need is urgent, and they know that, too.

Since its first great discoveries in the 15th and 16th centuries, science has been concentrated on what can be detected and measured, and that means the physical world, everything from minerals to microwaves and beyond. While it calls consciousness "the hard problem," it also expects to find its seat in the brain, and its fate in the mortality of the body.

Every time I ask her where she is, Anne says "I'm here." If I press her, she says, "Right here!"

So "here" must include more than I can see, hear, and taste and touch. But what would that be? This world is full of radio waves that we can't perceive, light in invisible frequencies, sounds that are too low or high for our ears to detect, smells that we can't perceive—in fact, the world is full of energies that elude the human senses.

All of the ones I have named, however, can be detected by scientific instruments. Anne is saying right now, this moment, that she's here. But I don't know of any instrument that can detect her.

My mind can hear her. Often, she says things so spontaneous and original that it's difficult for me to believe that I could have imagined them. But even those of us who do have contact with the nonphysical cannot provide material proof, not even to ourselves. What we generally have are signs such as the ones I've been reporting in these pages, sometimes quite startling, usually rather cryptic, and an inner voice of the loved one that might or might not originate in our own minds.

But, even as I am writing this, something has happened— or rather, reached a climax, and it is startling to me and deeply freeing and has changed my situation in fundamental ways.

Incredibly, Anne has managed to provide what for me on a personal level must be final proof. She has done something that at once goes to the heart of our relationship and also explores the deepest meaning of death, dying and living on. I will devote the final chapter of this book to it, but know that, from the time it happened just a few days ago, my position has changed. I now feel certain that Anne still exists, and with her I must also assume the legions of the dead, all still very real, but in ways that we have scarcely even begun to understand.

And yet, my innate skepticism persists with its questions. If they are as real as they now seem to me to be, then why can't they tell us what the president is doing, what planets harbor alien species, when we'll die?

Anne responds , "you see the world through a slit."

For a moment, the words sort of stun me. But then I think, 'yes, that's exactly right.'

But why would we be doing that? It would seem to be a tremendous disadvantage.

"Can we see more?"

"Some psychics already do, but it needs to be something everybody does."

"Because of the way things are changing?"

"Exactly. It's the first thing you find out when you come here. Then you realize that people can't hear you no matter how loud you shout. It's because we're less dense and faster. We can see you and hear you, but you can't perceive us."

"I sure perceive you."

"How well, though? Right now I'm kissing you but you can't feel it."

How I wish I could!

CHAPTER 6

Journey of Souls

SOME OF OUR website readers have reported contacts with Anne, and one of those reports might shed some light on the question of why we can't perceive those on the other side more clearly and fully.

This reader wrote that he had heard Anne say that she was returning to Earth by "going from blue to unguent blue." He was not clear about what this meant, but I saw it as another moment of valuable teaching, and it relates to why we can't interact with nonphysical being more coherently and reliably.

Anne was saying that she was in the higher vibration of light blue but moving to the darker, denser vibration of our world, explaining how the free souls move to contact those of us who are enclosed in physical bodies. The use of the word "unguent" is the key here. First, it means an ointment, that is to say, something more dense, as this world is more dense than the one above it. Also, though, it comes from Latin word, "to anoint," with its implication "to make sacred." It implies not only a movement from a lighter density to a heavier one, but also a touching of a kind that confers holiness—a healing touch from a higher world.

A kiss of objective love, such as I just received but could not feel.

To understand more deeply, we need to discuss the "why" of physical life. Why are we dense in the first place? Wouldn't we be better off if there was no physical side of our species at all? To somebody like Anne, it must be like scuba diving or dropping down into the abyssal deep in a submersible. Maybe it's even more difficult than that.

Unless physical life is some sort of prison, there can be only one logical reason for our being in such a condition: we need it like this. But why would we? I don't want to stumble through life as I do. I want to know my fate. I want to know how to avoid danger and tragedy.

Or do I?

If I knew what they dead know, my life would no longer hold the surprises that it does. A person in that state would never need courage or to appeal to conscience. Discovery would be impossible, revelation irrelevant.

The richness of surprise that fills the lives of those of us "looking through a slit" seems to me to be a treasure. Everything I have learned about myself has come from discoveries that depended on me knowing only enough of future, the past and the world around me to live in a continual state of surprise.

This limiting of vision is what gives life its impact. It causes us to act spontaneously, and therefore to look into the reasons for our behaviors and come to understand ourselves.

It is, in fact, the reason we are in physical form. Take it away, and one has no further reason to live as we do, blind to the future. So it's just as Anne said—we are indeed "intentionally ignoring" the nonphysical side of our species. In fact, I would assume that we're hard-wired to do it. We are like horses wearing blinders. We have no way of taking them off, for if we did, we would be overwhelmed with information about our true pasts and planned futures that would make our lives meaningless.

"Could you tell me things about the future that would disrupt my ability to learn from life?"

"I did at first. When I saw the world in such a new way, I just poured it out to you. I was so excited, it was incredible to see and know."

"Do you see everything—past, future?"

"We see what we are able. The more knowledge you bring, the more you can see. If they lived empty lives, people can be very minimal—just vague memories of themselves."

"You had a huge store of knowledge." "I did. I do."

"So tell me what's in store for me tomorrow?" She does not reply. "Well?"

"I did. Very clearly and in detail." "I didn't hear a thing."

"No."

"Could I have?"

"That's what we have to work on—widening and sharpening vision."

"Can you tell the future, then? Be a guide?"

"We can see what comes into focus earlier than you can, but nothing can be communicated that interrupts fate. I can tell you, but you won't hear me."

"Spirit guides?"

"Wisdom, yes. The future, no."

"You implied that your knowledge expanded when you died."

"It did. A lot. What you get is the ability to contemplate what you did in life. In the physical, we gather self knowledge. In the nonphysical, we seek to understand it."

"But if there's reincarnation, we must have already done this before."

"We often do it many times. Lives are brief and bodies are transitory, but souls are enormous, complex entities, each of them on a journey toward ecstasy that it would never, ever abandon. Something that big and nuanced can't finish its work in just a single lifetime. Most of us spend time between lives contemplating what we have done and planning our next journey. Not everybody, though. Some return right away, those who die in war, for example."

I recall the story of James Leininger who, as a toddler, recounted obscure details of a life that ended violently when he was a fighter pilot in World War II.

Incredibly, all the information he gave his parents turned out to be true even though it involved many incidents, ships and people who were too obscure to have entered history. He had the extraordinary experience of meeting in this life people he had known in his last one. The whole story is recorded in the book Soul Survivor.

He didn't ascend into a higher state or enter the all- encompassing light of objective love. Instead, he seems to have returned after a short time to this world, eager to complete the task he had set himself before his untimely death.

One reads in the near-death literature about that light that seems to absorb the soul into its loving and all-encompassing peace, but there must be many other states. Anne is still an intact, coherent being. In fact, preparing oneself to enter the state of coherence that she is in is a spiritual discipline that I practice every day of my life. That's one of the things the exercise I do is about.

I think that Anne came into life already in a state of soul coherence. Some ascend as Anne has, others enter the light, others linger nearby and get reborn. Maybe some even go to physical realities or other worlds and species entirely. Some also seem to descend into densities greater than this one.

I ask her, "How can we proceed here? What do I need to say to help people gain perspective about the aims of their own lives? And me too, for that matter? What do I need to know to improve the usefulness of my life experience to my soul?" "Let's do this stealthily. I'm not going to dialog with you.

Instead, I'm going to feed you ideas. They'll seem spontaneous, but they'll be coming from me."

"Is that common?"

"Yes, and it's not usually a good thing. It's called possession."

"I'd love to be possessed by you!" "You already are."

I quiet my thoughts. I listen.

I begin to find myself thinking about channeling, specifically about our experiences with a practitioner, Australian Glennys MacKay. She had channeled for us in such a way that it had proved to both of us that it had to be real.

After we met her and heard some of her claims, Anne decided to test her. She asked us to send her a lock of hair and she would 'read' it.

We were at our hairdressers a week or so later and it occurred to Anne to have him cut off a lock of his own hair to use in the experiment. There was no way in the world that Glennys could have guessed anything about this man. She had never met him or even heard of him and had no idea that it was his hair that arrived in an envelope from Anne a short time later.

Glennys reported that she had heard a woman's voice calling "Howie, Howie." As the hairdresser's name was Jay, we both assumed that she had failed.

However, when Anne told Jay what had happened, he was aghast. He said, "Anne, my real name is Howard. My dead sister always called me Howie."

When we heard this, we just fell silent. Anne said, "The dead call and call, and we don't hear." How ironic that she's doing that very thing right now and I'm the one she's calling. But there is a difference. I listen. I try hard to hear.

This was a very clean moment of mediumship. Glennys could not have plucked that information from Anne's mind. It wasn't there, not any of it. She didn't know Jay and we had no idea his real name was Howard. Just as what happened with Dr. Schwartz's medium and her hit on the Greek fisherman's hat, there is no avenue of information except contact between the medium and the dead person.

This does not mean that we understand what the dead are. Far from it. But we do know this: in some way, they are there. They must be.

A year later, Glennys and her husband arrived in Los Angeles on a trans-Pacific cruise. We were riding to a restaurant together when I asked Glennys, "Do you see the dead all the time?"

"Not all the time, but somebody dead is here right now.
With you."

I thought, 'ah, another chance to test.' I said, "Do tell." "He's wearing a tuxedo and playing a piano. No, now he's holding up a violin." She paused. "He says to tell you his name is Milton."

For an instant, I was blank. Then I remembered and when

I did I almost crashed the car. I had not thought of Milton A. Ryan, Jr. in at least thirty years. He had been the older brother of a boyhood friend, Mike Ryan, whose story figures in Ed Conroy's book about me, Report on Communion. He had not been a great part of my life, except for one thing. When he practiced the Beethoven Violin Concerto in his room and the notes had floated out across the neighborhood. His playing gave me a great gift, my lifelong love of classical music.

I had not been thinking of Mitty. In fact, I hadn't thought of him in all that time, not since his death in the early seventies. But here he was in the car with us, and she hadn't simply described him, she had given me his precise name.

This happened. Both events happened. On some level, I think that they were orchestrated to compel even resolute skeptics like the two of us to face the fact that channeling is real and the dead are still present and conscious.

I'm glad it happened, because now when I channel Anne I feel a sense of confidence I would not otherwise have.

Given that we have been exploring contact with the world of the dead in the west now for over two hundred years, it amazes me that so many of us are so resistant to this material, me included! It's as if we dare not embrace this reality, if only because we so badly want it to be true and so fear that it isn't.

Channeling probably started in the Scottish Highlands where "second sight" was a popular belief. Second sight practitioners, it was believed, could read the thoughts of others.

The first one to become well known was an 11 year old girl called Janet Douglas who, in the 1670s, began demonstrating her skills by revealing objects hidden by supposed witches and relieving people of the curses attached to them. She became a great sensation and was eventually sent before magistrates in Edinburgh on suspicion of being herself a witch. Shortly thereafter, she disappears from history, having apparently— and wisely—fled Scotland for the West Indies. The penalty for witchcraft in that time and place was to be burned alive.

Second sight remains very much part of the Scottish experience, with more than 10% of the overall population reporting it, primarily visions of future deaths. Most often this involves loved ones and friends, less often strangers. While this is not contact with the dead, it is related to the spiritualist movement that would develop in the 19th Century. But it is an event—or rather, the appearance of an individual

—in the late 18th Century that started the evolution of the modern concept of contact with the dead.

Swedish prophet and seer Emmanuel Swedenborg produced the first modern text specifically claiming to have been derived from contact with the dead and journeys into their reality. This was Heaven and Hell, published in 1758. In 1744, he'd had a spiritual awakening and thereafter sought to reform Christianity as essentially a spiritu- alist movement centered around contact between the living and the dead.

It was in the mid nineteenth century that channeling began to reach public attention. By that time, the idea of communication with the dead was spreading, and three sisters, Margaret, Kate and Leah Fox in upstate New York began making claims that they could effect it by a process that was called "spirit rapping," which is first mentioned in the early Scottish literature. As they were children when they began playing at this, it seems doubtful that they read any such accounts. Of course, it may have been discussed in the household.

The story of the sisters and their rapping spirits soon spread far and wide, and within a few years they were not only famous, but making a good living.

In the nineteenth century, with lifespans shorter and death a constant visitor in every household, the movement spread and became extremely popular. Soon, there was a lot of money involved and so also a lot of fraud. In fact, in 1888 one of the sisters, Margaret

Fox, told how as children they had created the rapping noises to fool their mother. They had used an apple tied to a string, dropping it on their bedroom floor at night. At first, they called the spirit they claimed to be in contact with "Old Splitfoot," but then later claimed it was a peddler called Charles Rosna, who had been murdered and whose body was buried in the cellar of their childhood home.

The Fox Sisters were dismissed as a fraud, but in 1904 a skeleton was indeed found buried in concrete in the cellar of the house, just as they had predicted.

The skeleton was very old, so it's unlikely that it was buried during the sisters' lifetime. Was it a household legend, and was that what inspired them to play their trick on their mother, or was the spirit of Charles Rosna somehow present and restless because of whatever befell him?

The way apparent fraud, even admitted fraud, works as part of this experience is complex. For example, right now in my life, I frequently hear unexplained rappings. I've been experiencing them for years, and they will often respond to simple questions. I don't make a practice of soliciting these rappings, but they do show up. In fact, one of the longest and most complex experiences I have had started every night for two years with seven loud thuds on the roof of my meditation room in the cabin that Anne and I owned in upstate New York. This involved an extensive contact with a group of people who claimed to be from between lives. It was no hoax and no misapprehension on my part, as I have reported in more detail in Solving the Communion Enigma.

What happened was that seven beings showed up at the cabin one night, dropping noisily onto the roof of the room where I meditated. For a moment, I wondered if opossums or raccoons were involved, but after the thuds there wasn't another sound.

I soon sensed their presence in the room. Without being able to see anybody in what now seemed a room full of people, I certainly couldn't meditate. I asked them to show themselves, but got no reaction. So I said that I'd have to see them if I was going to meditate with them and left the room.

Late that night, I was awakened to find a man sitting on the foot of our bed. I was terrified until I realized that he was no ordinary person. First, he was quite short. Second, he was wearing a tunic, not normal clothes.

I slid down to the foot of the bed. He was as slumped and still as a rag doll.

I looked right at him from a few feet away, right into his darkly shadowed eyes. Then I took his hand in mine. It was as light as that of a child, a little cooler than mine but not cold.

I held his hand and smelled his skin, and he seemed entirely human.

When I dropped his hand, he seemed to shudder as if shocked, then disappeared before my eyes.

The next night they came again. We meditated at eleven, then they woke me up at three and again at six. Each time, I would go down to the meditation room and sit and go deep. Their presence intensified my experience of the sensing exercise, and I began to feel as I do now, as if my sensation extended beyond the borders of my physical body and into the stuff of my soul.

We meditated together for months, night after night. It was among the most powerful and wonderful experiences of my life. During this time also, seven glowing plasmas were seen in our woods by a number of witnesses.

I felt as if we had raised our little cabin and the land around it to the edge of another reality. Truly, we were living at the edge of heaven. But our finances were also suffering and in October of that year we were faced with a choice: keep paying our mortgage and starve, or give up our beloved home.

Obviously, we had to go. But still they came, night after night, right up until the last night. I told them that I would never be here again, and also that I knew that I had never seen what they really looked like. I knew it wasn't just the plasmas or the physical form. I knew in myself that there was more.

On the last night, I asked to see the truth. I waited. Nothing happened. So I stood up and said goodbye and left that precious room forever.

I was lying in bed when I saw a glow in the front yard, along the side of the house. I rushed to the window. Slowly, majestically, a small star floated out the window of the meditation room and into the middle of the yard. Its rays were part of its life and as they touched my skin with gentle pricks, I felt the very essence of another human being. There were golden shapes in among the rays, and I knew that these were the emblems of past lives lived to such perfection that their memories had entered eternity.

That was a human being. It is what every one of us can become. All it takes is a willingness to live in love, to practice compassion and to be humble before all we meet. The burdens of anger, desire, regret and all the others will fall away, and there will be lightness of being, and ascension into ecstasy.

So we have the following: nightly rappings, a seemingly physical being, seven orbs of light and a star. I observed these things, and carefully. I am not mistaken about them. Anne came in one night and heard the thuds, but was not comfortable staying in the room to meditate with people she couldn't see.

Jeff Kripal comments in our book Super Natural, "I have studied religion for three decades now. I don't run into many new ideas. But this notion is shockingly new: the soul as a plasma like energy that can superpower our imaginal capacities and so generate the movies of visionary experience."

As I do, Jeff sees the experience as something unfolding within me. But also, I feel sure, it is outside of my body entirely, in the objective, real world. The beings were able to take many different forms—in fact, to control both their form and their density. When one of them became physical, I looked straight at him from a couple of feet away. I took his hand in mine and felt its solidity. But at the same time there was something subtly different about him. He was a material being, but it was a lighter material. I wouldn't think he had organs or blood.

Anne says it very well: "I'm a dream, but I'm also me."

Just as recent studies suggest that second sight in Scotland is something inherited genetically, I seem to have inherited my own tendency toward spirit contact, in my case probably from my mother's side of the family. One of my maternal great-grandmothers could generate table rappings and even cause heavy tables to hop and crack loudly. I sat in some of her séances and there was no fraud involved. As a skeptical teenager, I certainly looked for it, peering under the table and actually watching her feet and legs as the rappings came rattling out of the tabletop. She did not move.

So I'm not prepared to dismiss mediumistic rappings as simple fraud. Rapping may or may not involve contact with the dead, but it isn't all hoaxed. What happened at the cabin was also no hoax and was, in fact, one of the most intimate experiences of contact with the dead that I think has ever been recorded.

Unlike the ectoplasm that came out of the mouths of 19th Century mediums and was generally regurgitated cheesecloth and other substances, the plasmic being who sat on the foot of my bed was entirely real. He was not a mental construction but a physical entity about four feet tall, sitting there slumped against the bed's footboard in a tunic. When I smelled his hand, the skin was ripe. This man was not only real, he was not somebody who bathed.

I looked right at him. There was the unmistakable sense of a physical presence. But when I dropped his hand, he disappeared in a wink. I think this happened because it was taking all the attention he possessed to maintain his memory of his body as a physical presence. When I suddenly let go of the hand, the need to simulate the movement was too much—he could not maintain balance anymore and, as it were, fell up into his normal—and higher—vibration.

I know that these are extremely unusual experiences, but I am describing them as accurately as I am able. They happened. It's that simple. And to me they mean that the dead are still with us and even that they can, under certain circumstances and perhaps needing specialized skills, manifest a physical presence.

The great-grandmother who could move tables was a Swedenborgian. She used to say to me, "After I die, listen to the wind in the trees. That's how I'll speak to you." She was a noted school teacher in San

WHITLEY AND ANNE STRIEBER

Antonio with an excellent reputation for taking a very empirical approach in her professional work. But in private she explored other domains with panache.

She lived to the age of 106, and after she died, I listened for her when the wind sighed in the night trees, but never heard her promised whispers, or perhaps I tuned them out.

In all of our past efforts to reconnect with our dead and in all cultures, there is a missing element which is probably essential to real success. The dead do not need to be called by any special techniques. The essential element is not skill, it's love—that is to say, the creative power of objective love. This love is a principle, I think, of a higher physics than that of the material world. Just as certainly as gravity, which holds the material world together, it is a fundamental attractor. Learning to live in this state of objective love—wanting the universe, the world and all life to be—is crucial to connecting with one's own dead. They don't need to be given sacrifice or worshiped, but rather to be enjoyed for their lives and presence, just as they were when in the physical state.

My contact with the dead began at my grandmother's funeral in 1976. Although she was the daughter of a Swedenborgian, in her life, I never heard her make serious reference to spiritualism. But, like many of us in the family, she had seen ghosts and participated in her mother's séances, which entertained three generations of our family.

There was a large congregation, and her coffin rested in the aisle of the church. I was in a pew just behind it when, to my surprise, I saw six large, softly glowing balls of light come sliding gracefully in through the ceiling and array themselves around the coffin.

They appeared entirely real to me, but I was also aware that nobody else was reacting to them. I thought, 'they're souls.' Then I knew that they were there because my granny did not believe that she was dead. She had been determined to live as long as her mother, and was still in her body in the coffin. They were trying to get her to come out.

I wanted to help, but I couldn't see how. After a while, the six souls soared gracefully upward and were gone. They did not float. They moved with a precision that was startling to see, it was so perfect and so accurate.

This was the beginning of what has become a lifetime of contact with the dead. In this particular case, it went on for years. My grandmother was not finally freed from the bonds of this life until the late 1980s.

Right after she died, I saw her in my mind's eye sitting in a room in her house telling a group of patient listeners about all the wonderful homes she had created. She had exquisite taste and had, in fact, created some lovely places. I sensed, though, that she was still entirely unaware that she was dead.

A couple of years later, I saw her again. This time, she was standing before a lovely and elaborate house. I called to her, but she would not turn around. Then, at least ten years after that, I saw her again. Now, only the front of the house remained, just the part that she was staring at, red brick with roses climbing up the walls. Again, I called to her. This time, she turned. She looked at me curiously. As she did so, her eyes slowly turned to gold. Then she darted upward and was gone at last from her remembering and her dreams, finally free.

I will not see her again, I wouldn't think. She was not like Anne, a person with a mission here. Maybe she will return to the physical. Maybe she already has. But there are many paths in the land of consciousness. All I know is that wherever she is, love is there, too, as it is everywhere that being is, the found, the lost, the wanderers and the seekers, it does not matter. This greater love—objective love—simply is. It sees reality from the outside and yet also fills it in every nook and cranny. It allows without necessarily accepting, and that is why it is so fundamentally different from the idea known as 'unconditional love,' which, as a form of sentimentality, both allows and accepts.

You can feel it. We all can. When I do the sensing exercise, I let myself also feel this urgency, this wanting that is objective love. My subjective feelings of joy, love, anger, hate, compassion—all of that—are not ignored but rather are seen as part of objective love, like everything that is, wanted.

I feel myself as a humble part of a greater whole, and let awe and joy carry me into the sweet, expansive state that is higher awareness.

So one can let one's own love join objective love as a humble part of the whole. If you do that, then even though you are still just a little person struggling along on this Earth, you are also all love everywhere, beyond time and pain.

Encounters with souls that are stuck in one way or another is a commonplace of any life that is lived in communion with the nonphysical level of humanity. As we become more skilled in managing our relationships with our dead, we are going to find them all around us.

When I was meditating during the summer of 2017 in an old house in Italy, I watched a woman in a black skirt and loose-fitting blouse move slowly around the room dusting furniture that was no longer there. I watched her for a long time and tried to get her attention, but she dusted and dusted. Finally, she walked off into another part of the building. How long she might have been doing this I cannot tell, but she obviously still sees the same world she lived in. She should be called a ghost, I suppose, but I see them as spirits who are simply unaware that they have lost their way.

To help them, you have to go out of your own body or raise its vibration so that you can touch them and turn them, and send them on their way. When you try to do this, you'll find that you can. We all know how. This is because we also have instinctive knowledge at the soul level.

Those trapped in the physical wander. They have no idea where to go or what to do. The heavy ones fall like tears

forgotten. Some like Anne ascend, then turn around to face life from their new perspective, seeking to help tend this garden.

Others rise and rise, seeking beyond the stars toward the expanding border of consciousness, the limit of ecstasy. I hunger for this myself. I feel it in me. I sense what it is, ascension: a new song that I—and all of us—have always known.

CHAPTER 7

"The Living Will Know the Dead"

As Planet Earth changes, our fragile technological societies become ever more vulnerable, and our huge populations with them.

I am not speaking so much of short term changes such as global warming, but rather of the much larger cycle which is going to happen regardless of any human effect. Either we will go into another glaciation or a long period of warming. Both have happened in the past, and it's not clear which will happen now. But one thing is clear: climate is changing.

So how should we prepare?

There can potentially be all sorts of technological fixes and scientific solutions, but this book is not about that.

Previously we made reference to tools—the tools of the soul. It is these tools that are involved in the kind of preparation we are concerned with here. They are inner tools, and we already posses them. It's a question of opening the inner door behind which we conceal them from ourselves, taking them out and making use of them.

We need help doing that, though. We need the wisdom of our dead, and this could be why, over the past two centuries, there has been such a marked change in their relationship with us.

Their attempt to reach us would explain the rise of the medium movement, the appearances of more and more psychics and now the afterlife revolution. These things are the human species attempting to increase its production of strong souls and increased its overall intelligence and predictive abilities by reconnecting its two halves.

Let me describe how this is working for Anne and me right now, as I am writing.

I feel her close to me. She wasn't close earlier this morning, but she has become aware that I'm writing and is now a definite presence near me and, to an extent, within me.

I accept this but also don't abandon the question. While I am functioning as if Anne is Anne and is right here, but I am asking if it's really her or if I am communicating with my idea of her, and I am accepting that it is probably part of both. I am communicating with the Anne in my mind and heart, and also with Anne in the afterlife.

It would help if there was physical manifestation, of course, but there has so far been only one of these. On that occasion, when she finished speaking to me in a particularly intense way, full of the speed and spontaneity of physical conversation, I glimpsed a small light go flashing away out of our apartment.

She had been here and close because of something she wanted to say. After she created our website in 1999, she began posting the occasional entries on it she called "Anne's Diary." About six months after she left the physical, I heard her saying that she wanted to continue it.

I sat down, quieted my mind and opened it to her. I did this by doing the sensing exercise. As it draws the attention away from the mind and onto the body, it opens the mind to outside influences.

At once, thoughts flew through my mind. They were so fast and so spontaneous that they really did not feel like my own. It was exactly as if somebody else was talking in my head. And they were. Anne was.

If I tried to listen, they were pushed aside by my own thoughts. I solved that problem by jotting notes, and in a few minutes I had a whole, complex statement written down, one that was original and wise and beautiful. In it, I could almost hear Anne's gentle, insistent voice.

I posted the entry, pretty much quoting her word for word, on February 16, 2017 as "Anne's Valentine to You: 'We are Lovers.'"

In it, she says, "We have trouble believing what is real even when it's staring us right in the face, especially if it's not what we want to be true. But we do have something that makes us special. We are lovers, and in this respect we stand out as a very remarkable achievement of our planet and its star."

I say to her now, as I am writing, "I'm glad that we have something to recommend us, but I'm more interested in this problem of seeing what's real. That's why we can't communicate with you reliably. That's what we need to change."

Anne: "With no physical points of reference it's always going to be hard for you to accept us. I also don't think it's healthy to do that uncritically. The key is a stable attention, strong enough to keep your mind empty of thought so we can enter it. The mind flutters around like a little moth, drawn here and there at random."

"That's what I did to hear the diary. But I want to know how to strengthen it."

"Go to a quiet place, do the sensing exercise, listen and take notes without thinking about them. Not automatic writing, though. Open yourself to directed thought from the outside."

"In other words, channel."

"Exactly. It's the process we've been teaching you for two hundred years. Remember that every time somebody channels in one life, they're better at it in the next. That's what our school is all about: multi-generational teaching."

"Remember the study we made of prophecies, when we were researching channeling?" We had found that spirit guides did not do well at foretelling the future.

"Now I know why guides turn out to be such bad prophets.

They're not like us, not on this level. They're with you, and they don't know any more than you do about the future. So they guess. A spirit guide is generally no more prophetic than the person channeling her."

"But you know more?"

"To a surprising degree the future is an open book." "Could you meditate with us, then? That might help us." "Getting to you is like swimming really deep. It feels like

getting lost. There's no exit. You feel like you could end up among the wanderers who can't find their way out."

"It's frightening?"

"It's difficult. But when the glow that comes from the sensing exercise starts, it's much easier. We can focus on that light and get right to you."

"What about the dead who show up with the visitors?

What's going on there?"

"The ones you and I call the visitors are practiced at moving between densities. When they tunnel down into your density, the human dead can follow them, or they can be brought. This is being done to make those of you in the physical aware that we still exist. It's part of the fight against soul blindness and it's also the foundation of bridge building."

I ask, "So what happens now? Where are they taking us?"

"Higher and higher into ecstasy, as you've always said." "But terrible things happen and are going to happen. That

doesn't seem to me like a journey into ecstasy."

"Pain forms a foundation of strength. Remember your story."

In early 1986 I wrote a short story called Pain that was about an angel causing a man to experience pain that frees him from his past and causes him to see life anew. A new vision, brighter, more fruitful, comes to him when he accepts the pain and goes past it.

She responds, "Out of the coming age of upheaval there is going to emerge either a new humanity or no humanity."

I pause, letting the stark frankness of that statement penetrate. I have always known that the stakes in our era were very high, but not until this moment did I have a real understanding of just how high.

"Earth's surface is a womb. In this womb, a baby, life, has been growing for eons. This baby has matured to the point that it has intellect and therefore the capacity to enter higher consciousness—that is, to be born. So the waters of Earth's womb are breaking."

I understand this all too well. When Earth's waters break, as they are now doing, mankind—her baby—will no longer have the support of the womb. Like it or not, the baby is going to be born, and into a completely new life.

Anne says, "We will still have a physical presence, but not nearly as large a one as we do now. So souls will need to be more efficient. They will have to enter bodies to accomplish specific tasks of self-discovery. It cannot be random anymore, not if everybody is going to get all the chances they need."

"I'm not sure I understand."

"After the transformation of the planet, there will still be souls entering physical bodies, but the experience will be different. The whole species is going through a gigantic shamanic initiation. The seeker enters death in order to experience life in a new and more encompassing way. The outcome of this initiation will be that the blinders of physical life will be removed, randomness and chance will no longer play so much of a role in life as they do now, and souls will enter bodies with knowledge of their reasons for doing so intact. The living will know the dead. They will no longer be wanderers like the fool in the Tarot, but users of the tools of consciousness, like the Magician with his bundle open on the workbench before him."

But don't make any assumptions when you see the word "Tarot." It is an ancient psychological system that references body, mind and soul, not just body and mind as modern psychology does. And that is how Anne and I use it, not as a means of divination. I have laid this out in a little book called the Path.

I say to her, "I want to know more about his tools."

"The tools that strengthen the soul are understanding and living in objective love, engaging in the sensing exercise and meditation to strengthen the soul, and practicing love, compassion and humility to free it from the bondage of ego. Those are the basics."

"That's the basic message of the gospels."

"It's the basic message of all religions. It is the message of man."

It is also the reason that the afterlife revolution can now take place. Nonphysical mankind, along with many different

sorts of midwives and helpers, is preparing physical mankind for the shock of species initiation, and to use our planet afterward in a new way. To be born to the world is to die to the womb. On exiting the birth canal, the infant enters on a new life, and so does the mother. There is no return, not for either of them.

The mysterious presences that are here with us know this. They have lived it. Having been through the sort of birth that we are now facing, they are here as midwives. The mother may find the midwife a comfort and a blessing, but in the baby's confused perception as it emerges from the womb she appears to be a raucous, dangerous and monstrous presence, ferocious and frightening. But then there is something else, a bond to mother that baby feels but does not understand. The baby focuses on this bond so completely that the mother becomes everything to her.

This is very different from the baby's time in the womb. During that period, the baby took everything for granted, food, comfort, safety—all these things were provided.

Once outside, though, baby begins to see mother as a separate being. He perceives that he is dependent on this mother of his, and stops taking things for granted. When the mother feeds him and comforts him, he falls in love, as we will with our own planet. We will at last come to see her as a living being with hopes and dreams, not simply as a passive lump of nutrients there to serve us in silence.

The mother, who has loved the baby in her womb out of instinct will now join it in a state of conscious love. A relationship between mother and child will form. We will see that our planet has awareness and needs and will come

to regard her not only as our home, but also as our dear and beloved friend.

Anne: "All through history, there have been those who have lived in conscious relationship with Earth and cosmos. We call them masters. In the future, everybody who enters the physical will do so as a master of being. And why will we still be using the physical? Give somebody a kiss. That's why. Humanity's destiny in the universe is to bring forth the experience of love, that all may share in it. Objective love, the core creative urgency, is also the essential human energy."

Love, again. It always comes back to this missing element, the unseen strength that will see us through even the most difficult of times. "Love one another," said by one of those masters of whom Anne speaks.

This is, after all and above all, a book of love. But love as a power, a force in the universe. Gravity draws matter together and keeps things whole. Love draws us together, and urges us to seek higher and deeper, into the realms of joy that are our destination.

CHAPTER 8

A New Vision of Life

I ONCE MET a person from a species that has been through the valley we are now entering, and living as we will if we emerge from it. At the time, I didn't fully understand what I was experiencing, but over the years I have learned more about the way souls—and species—evolve and what living a good life really means. It is not living in empty sweetness, but taking the good with the bad—embracing the light of life, learning from what we find in the dark.

"I didn't understand that when you told me about it, either, but now it's clear to me, too."

We were at a hotel in San Francisco attending a conference. At about midnight, I was meditating in the living room of our little suite. The next thing I knew, there was a young woman standing before me. She had a northern-European face and complexion. Looking back, I seem to remember that she had eyes as green as emeralds. Green—the color of acceptance and also of rebirth. I see it now as a reminder that we must experience what is unfolding in our world, but also that afterward there will be a new birth.

The young woman was wearing the most wonderful dress I had ever seen. It was a living thing, not a piece of cloth. As I looked at it in astonishment, I saw that it was decorated with thousands of scenes, like tiny, incredibly detailed paintings. But they were not paintings, they were living moments. They moved, as if all of these incidents were happening right now, all at once.

The dress carried scenes of her life as they would be observed from outside of time. Every one of them radiated a poignant joyousness, as if each was the sweetest moment that had ever been. But I could see that there were dark scenes there, too, amid the flowers and the blue.

She radiated a goodness so intense that my soul went out of my body to get closer to it. And there I was, fluttering at her feet. She looked down at me, nonplussed and embarrassed.

I had just enough time to feel like an idiot before my son came rushing in. "Dad," he cried, "there's a big silver flying saucer outside my window."

Instantly, she was gone and I was back in my body. I ran into his room, but there was nothing outside but the night.

Anne says, "You were seeing what we can become. That's the next state after this one."

"Have joy?"

"Exactly. A joyous and accepting heart. You saw her life journeys. Even though not all of them were pleasant, she experienced every one with joy. You were seeing her from outside of time."

"She was enlightened, then?"

"Enlightenment is what happens when there is nothing left of us but love."

"Were you enlightened while you were physically alive?"

"When you're enlightened in one life, die and enter another, you're still enlightened. Death and rebirth don't turn that light off."

"You seemed just normal."

"Enlightenment is normal. Pretending that it's special is what's not normal. That's why that kid was so embarrassed. She was just there to offer some knowledge. She didn't expect to be worshiped."

"We're all enlightened?"

"Accepting yourself is the key. Enjoying yourself."

Anne enjoyed herself every moment she could. She enjoyed her mind, her heart, her body. (I did, too, for that matter!) To my wife, life was a continuous and unfolding miracle. For her, consciousness was a matter of noticing all the details of life, and she was wonderful at it.

"Also, species in the state humankind is entering—living as we do and that girl does, outside of time looking in—have new opportunities to find joy, and with them new responsibilities. The child is born, grows up, leaves the mother's side and goes out into the world to find his own life. And marriage. That, too, and children, even that."

"We'll have children as a species? I'd never thought of that."

"Everybody is somebody's child. We'll go out in the universe just like others do and find worlds full of scuttling creatures out of whom we can make new minds."

I think a long time about this. It reminds me of an idea I proposed in Solving the Communion Enigma, that we might eventually play the same role with another species that the visitors play with us. But this is a bigger version of that idea. It suggests a rich and unexpected future for us, and certainly makes it clear why others might be here trying to midwife our birth.

I remember so fondly the evenings of long ago when Anne and I would sit on the deck at our cabin and speculate about the meaning of this journey of being. Anne was the one who understood the situation and knew why our visitors—at least the ones who were involved with us—were here. She saw so clearly the towering possibilities that lie before us.

But look at the promise her idea of our future contains— that we may be able to join a vast communion, the presence of which we are now almost entirely unaware. More, that we may become shepherds, helping others in the future as we are being helped now.

What would it be like to be somebody else's gods? They would be like children gazing up at us in awe, and we would be like our visitors, tired and scared and working hard.

Perhaps ten years ago, maybe more, an image appeared in my mind during meditation. It was of a slow, wide river. I was looking down into a boat where a small figure sat huddled over a fishing rod, his back to me. As I looked down at him, a glow appeared on the water. He sat up, stared, then turned to see its source. He looked up at me carefully, as if he was seeing something that he didn't understand but also didn't see as a threat. And then it ended. I was back in my living room, my mediation once again normal.

Did he see a glowing orb, perhaps, that was me? Is that how I appeared to him? I wonder what he made of it and how he described to others what he had beheld. I also wonder if we will ever meet again, perhaps many hundreds of years from now, when mankind has become for his species in their distant world the spirit moving on the waters, struggling to help them be born as we are being born now, into the light of objective love.

If we do our job well, they will say, "it happened to us naturally," as the people say of the actions of the best king in the Tao Te Ching. As our own visitors will when their work is done, we will slip away into the firmament and be gone from their lives.

When we find them, they will be living as we are now, in a state of separation between physical and nonphysical sides— as it were, an immature species.

They will be at the point of birth out of their own mother planet, just as we are right now. We will become their "aliens," offering them support and schooling from our own experience. Doing midwifery like this is the next stage in our collective journey into the state of ecstasy that the woman who appeared in my hotel room was in. From what I have seen of our own visitors, this midwifery is a real challenge, too, exhausting and frustrating but, I suspect and hope, worth the effort.

Anne: "Birth doesn't necessarily have to work, you know. There are no guarantees. We could be "born dead," that is to say, in a state of such chaos that we may never fully recover from it. Never forget that the baby doesn't see what's at stake, only the midwife. You're fixated on these "other" beings acting as midwife. Seek deeper. They are like us and part of us. Forget the idea of aliens versus humans, angels versus demons. These ideas are not big enough to fit reality. There are no aliens. No humans. Only us. No good, no evil—only us again, making our choices."

I think she means not that "they" are or are not from other planets, but that this sort of difference is irrelevant to the experience of being conscious. Of course, different brains compile different visions of the world, but above the physical level, in nonphysical consciousness, all vision is objective and inclusive.

"Graduating into the next level, where we will be a teacher for others, is only a small part of growing up as a species. Consciousness is a journey into joy, which is without end. After you leave your body for the final time, this is the first thing you remember. And you think —at least I did—how could I ever have forgotten this? Your ego disappears, just like that, and when it does you see, Whitley, you really see. We live in a huge world that we hide from ourselves. As I left my body, "Anne" became a memory. You're you, but also everybody. It's really a warm, joyous moment."

"It sounds like disappearing."

"Ego dies, not self. We need to rethink our idea of body and soul. It's not entirely right to think of them as being separate. There is only one person. We exist on a continuum of densities. Over time, we shed these densities. Just as you won't be physical forever, I won't be in my current state forever. And the less dense we become, the more holographic we are. This is the surrender to God that adepts like Meister Eckhart describe. As he puts it, we 'become as a clear glass through which God can shine.' As our world becomes unable to support us, we are going to need to surrender ourselves into that greater truth."

"How?"

"'Two are better than one, and a cord of three strands is not quickly snapped.' Remember that? In the physical, that cord is our kids. In my density, it's the silver cord you saw stretching between us as I left your level."

She is quoting from Ecclesiastes 4: 9-12 here. Back in 1970, chose that as the motto of our marriage and made a cross-stitched sampler of it. To this day, that sampler hangs on our bedroom wall. The third strand is our son who is carrying us on, and also the harmony between us that is eternity in our marriage.

The hours after Anne left this life revealed to me the strength of that cord, which I now see as the fundamental binding between the physical and nonphysical sides of the species, and the one thing that we can count on never to break.

What she and I are doing together, and what it is possible for any two people who have surrendered to love to do, is summed up in Card XXI of the Major Arcana of the Tarot. The twenty-first card is called "the World." On it, a being that

is both man and woman ascends in a wreath of laurel, symbolic of their victory.

On the four corners of the card are pictured the four keys to attaining objective love. These are the four beasts of the sphinx, a triad in balance. Instinct, emotion and mind are working together objectively, without identification with desires, fears and needs. Objective love is the fourth beast, the eagle, who soars above life and sees it from the distance that the dead experience, a distance that lends objectivity.

When one lives like this, in this state, one becomes free of the idea that the body is all we have. People do not seem to be just bodies, but rather bodies come to appear as coatings that contain souls. The coating, the body, is a mechanism that the real person—the soul—uses to navigate physical reality.

Living with a vision of oneself and others like that is a great freedom that leads to deeper understanding of a kind that prepares us for any shock, any change, because we are always that crucial hair's breadth behind the shocks that the body is enduring. No matter how desperate the situation, the watcher retains the power of reflection.

We the living are generally absorbed in ego, and because ego dies with the body, we are terrified of death. People like Anne, who didn't live that way, don't find death frightening at all. Like her, they see it as

93

a transition, which is one of the most empowering things that they can teach us from their nonphysical perspective.

For example, the presence I call Anne is not the person I knew in this life. She holds that personality between us so that I can recognize her, but it is not her true being. Even though

Anne is now a memory, she is not gone. Personality echoes essence, though, so even when I glimpse my dear teacher in her true expression, what I see is someone who makes sense as the foundation of the person I knew in physical life.

I find myself returning once again to the man who materialized before me. If that could happen in a regular, verifiable way, it would solve many of the problems of communication, not to mention finally curing the disease of soul blindness.

"What makes materialization possible?"

"You have to be able to get energy to organize itself like matter. It takes tremendous concentration and skill."

"It's too rare!"

"That's why they make you do the sensing exercise so much. The more you do it, the more coherent your soul becomes. When you lose your body you don't lose your focus. You can come back."

"Will I be able to do that?" "That's the hope."

I think about that. Will it happen? It seems completely impossible, and yet I have seen it done.

"Why did those people come to just me? Why not thousands of people? Millions?"

"People don't notice."

"Why not?"

"Ego filters out what it fears, and what it fears most of all is death."

I remember how terrifying the visitors were at first. I could feel it in my blood that they had something to do with death. "If ego is that afraid, what can we do?"

"Strengthen humility. Fear of death comes from ego. A humble person lives from the part of themselves that is immortal. They accept death naturally instead of fearing it."

"Which is exactly what you did."

"I put down the burdens of desire and anger, judgment and self-importance, all of that, and there I was still in my body but behind Anne. I was my soul, not my personality, and knew for certain that there was nothing to fear."

And there it is—the state we need to find within ourselves in order to navigate the coming drama of our birth. But how? What are we to do?

CHAPTER 9

Soul Tools

THE YOUNG WOMAN I saw had a highly evolved soul. But why, and how had she come to be that way?

We discussed the soul tools in the last chapter, but how do we use them? We can't see the soul. We can't even feel it. When one does the sensing exercise, little happens. The mind is quiet for a few moments here and there during the session. Almost always, though, there's little else.

So, are there changes? Anything?

The visitors Anne and I work with are experts at soul building, and they have given us plenty of advice. The first thing to understand is that we identify ourselves as our egos, but that isn't who we are. Ego is a brain function and as such mortal. It develops around the name we are given at birth. It is a social tool that the brain uses to interact with other people.

When a person goes soul blind, ego rushes to fill the vacuum. Being out of touch with the soul, it becomes obsessed with the survival of the body. We find ourselves living in constant, unspoken terror of death.

But when one learns the art of deepening the sensing exercise enough to include the soul, this changes. Ego fear is accepted as a natural side effect of its mortality. The soul is not afraid of death. It has no reason to be. But how do we even begin to see the world through the eyes of the soul?

I ask Anne, "We have a sort of anesthesia about the soul. We don't feel it. So of course we cling to ego and live in terror of death. How can we change this?"

I feel her laugh the big, deep laugh always seemed so improbable coming out of a small person like her.

"I don't understand"

Then I do. She saw laughter as a key to consciousness— in fact, as the key. Her message of "have joy" I cannot repeat enough. She says, "When you ascend, you ascend into laughter. You can't understand the big bang unless you understand it as an explosion of happiness. The instant that consciousness realized that it was alone, it laughed with surprise. That was the beginning of everything, soul laughter."

Ego can laugh, but not like that. This is because ego can never experience the innocence of objective love and happiness. This is happiness that is too simple for ego to know. It is the happiness of little children and why Jesus was always using them as examples. It is the happiness of my wife.

I remember once we were in the Italian town of Siena. We'd been traveling all day and we were hot and tired. To our surprise, we discovered a wonderful big Jacuzzi in our hotel room. Anne got in it and rolled in the warm water with a smile of absolute delight on her face. It was the open smile of a baby. She lived in an innocence that I have never in all my adult life tasted, not with all my inner work. But it was just her—the way she was.

"Do you wear a dress like that girl?"

Then it hits me—another realization about the way this text is being constructed. Last night I had a rather mysterious dream. I was with Anne and we were looking at clothes. There were lovely knitted dresses in the store, very colorful, and I was sure she would like them. But she didn't. She said, "I'm already in my dress."

I didn't think to look at her and now I could kick my thick old hide for it!

I could have seen her from outside of time last night, and tasted of the whole wonder of her being, and I missed my chance!

But I also know from long experience that this was a good soul lesson. Ego blocked my innocence, which is why I couldn't see hers. It has needs and desires, disappointments and failures. But we're inside it. We see the world through it. We see ourselves and others through it.

"It also locks your expectations. Move your attention away from personality and into body and the key will turn, the door will open and you will come new."

"You can't destroy ego."

"Nor should you try. Ego is your key social tool."

"You didn't always live in ego." "Not always."

She could laugh her ego right out of her way and then there she was grinning from ear to ear—her soul.

"That's it, laughter!"

The place to start on this sweet work of letting ego go is to take ourselves more lightly. Ego cannot observe itself objectively. It cannot understand itself or hold a mirror up to itself. But the soul can understand it, for the soul was present at its creation and has observed it throughout all of the body's life.

When you get to the bottom of everything you consider most serious in your life, all the disappointments and injustices and misfortunes, the loves, the needs and the hopes, you find that same quiet, bubbling, joyous presence that I would often see in Anne and occasionally even find in myself. And that's your soul. That's how it feels.

But to realize this, we must first go beyond the conventional definition of "soul." If we think of it at all, we might vaguely imagine an echo of what we can see of ourselves, that is to say, ego. I have even heard people speak of "afterlife ego" and "soul ego." But soul is not ego and it isn't similar to ego. Truly, our souls are undiscovered countries.

They at once lie within us and live in all being and all time, knots of consciousness that have a definite sense of self, a definition that is all their own, but equally a sense of conscious infinity.

The moment the attention comes out of ego and enters soul, it sees the personality from the outside. It sees the body and all its parts as its own temporary container. Later, it also comes to see that it isn't actually in the container, not completely, but rather is more like a puppet-master manipulating the marionette of self from a perch high above.

When I go to this state, the first thing that tells me that I am drawing near is a rising sense of mirth.

"There's laughter here," Anne says. "It's the first and most creative force. That's what too many people forget. They forget that the holy of holies is joy." And not just them. How little laughter there is in our world.

Meister Eckhart is one of the few religious leaders who understood the power of laughter. He said, "Do you want to know what goes on in the heart of the Trinity? I will tell you. In the heart of the Trinity the Father laughs and gives birth to the Son. The Son laughs back at the Father and gives birth to the Spirit. The whole Trinity laughs and gives birth to us."

But why? What's so funny?

Consciousness has set out to discover all knowledge, that's what. So did Don Quixote. Riding his ass is so much fun, though, that nobody ever thinks of getting off. On the back of this ass, you go everywhere and nowhere at the same time. Contradictions abound, and yet they also make sense. The more conscious you become, the more playful you feel.

This is what is meant by the Meister's comment that "God laughs and plays."

Anne always maintained that "God laughs and plays" was the best thing about the sacred that anybody has ever said.

Meister Eckhart in his life was called a man who knew God. Anne did, too, and laughed about it just as much.

I guess that's also why Quag showed up during that meditation of mine instead of some awesome figure with a fiery glare. He knew that

I was with a friend of his, a fellow traveler on the laughter road, who would understand who he was and why he appeared as he did and teach me.

But why is laughter so creative? It reacts to contradiction with delight is why, thus opening the road to new discoveries. This allows mysteries to open like flowers, and what seems a prison—this life— becomes a palace of question and surprise and the deliciousness of discovery. And when the clouds are flying and the house is trembling, that is still true and true more than ever.

Life doesn't feel that way, though. Life feels hard and unfair and dangerous. Our physical instincts tell us to see others as enemy or friend, evil or good. We divide the world, and ourselves, much too simply. By identifying things in this way we lose sight of what they really are. We deny the soul it's chance to gain access to our attention, because the soul cannot perceive the world in this way. The rages and disappointments, lusts and triumphs of ego are a wall that stands between us and our souls. Caught behind that wall, you can't see the bridge beyond, or hear the dead, shouting themselves silly from the far side.

None of us can really hear, not very well. So let's look at the journey through these pages as building for the future. Remember that ego and soul both read the same words. They just read them differently.

Because we have divided ourselves into physicalists and dualists, we have also ended up thinking of the soul as being something that somehow lives in the body as a sort of separate entity, or that it isn't there at all. Anne is right, though, when she says that's not the way to go about it.

We have a long history of looking at the soul as something sepa-rate from us but within us. Descartes theorized that it was in the pineal gland, because that gland is at the center of the brain. But it's not there. In one way, the physicalists are right: the soul isn't anywhere. It is part of the body in the same sense that color is part of paint. As Anne says, "Paint fades but color is immortal." When she described to our reader how it felt to move between the two densities of blue when entering and leaving the physical state, she was giving him the chance to see our world not as ego does—as an entanglement of beings, events and objects, but rather from the objective standpoint of the soul—the soaring eagle—who sees it not only as all those captivating details, but also as a density, that is to say a color of a certain shade.

But how can you possibly see life in that way—not as events and all the identifications that go with them, but simply as color? In other words how do we step away from the details far enough to spread the wings of objective love and rise above the riotous surface?

It turns out that it's simpler than the many weighty tomes on the subject would suggest. In fact, ridiculously so.

Let's take a closer look at love, compassion and humility. Love innocently, find compassion always and live a humble, simple life and you will emerge a pure soul. Your vibratory color will be, as Anne puts it, "azure."

Like all manifesting energy, the three pillars of the soul are a triad. Love is the active side and humility the passive. Compassion creates balance between the two. But compassion, like all balancing forces, is hard to understand. It isn't simply giving a dollar to a hobo, but understanding what all with whom we come into contact need the most from us, and what we need to give ourselves. In the Gurdjieff work, it is said that we are "third force blind." Until you can give up being a judge of yourself and others, you cannot begin a search into compassion.

In the gospels, there are many examples of it. When Jesus suffered the little children, when he told the story of the Good Samaritan— these are stories about compassion. But also the story of how he overturned the tables of the moneychangers in the temple is about compassion. But how was compassion involved in what appears to be an expression of outrage? The answer is that he was giving the bankers a chance to see their greed and perhaps step back and review the direction of their lives.

With regard to humility, the sternest lessons I have received in the school of the visitors involve this soul tool.

Many years ago, my brother had come up to our cabin. I was feeling a lot of pride, showing him around, showing off my material achievements. Then, as I was taking him to see the place where my ascension into the presence of the visitors had occurred, I heard a voice say, "Arrogance. I can do whatever I wish to you."

It was the lady on the cover of Communion. I thought, ' surely this is my imagination,' but told myself to quit my bragging.

When we got to the clearing, we saw a lovely, bright UFO slip elegantly across the sky. Then I thought, 'oh, dear, it wasn't my imagination.'

I was worried. I had already discovered that the school of the visitors is intense because it is about the health of the soul, and the soul is eternal.

I could expect a hard lesson, and indeed, that's just what unfolded the next morning. My bank called to say that they had a number of checks I'd written, but I had no account with them.

She'd made my damn money disappear! Talk about an ego lesson! I had just a few dollars in my pocket, now the only money I possessed in the world. Worse, those checks would be bounced if my account couldn't be restored by the close of business. Desperately, I pleaded with the bank manager to look for the account in their computer. Later, I drove over and sat with him while he searched. He found nothing. Finally, he agreed to give me another day and said he would look in the bank's magnetic records.

In the event, they found the account in the Iron Mountain records storage facility where the bank kept its emergency backup files. Everything else had been erased. As the manager put it, "Nothing like this has ever happened before."

No, I would think not.

I have never forgotten that lesson. I wouldn't dare brag that I've lived a humble life ever since, but I have surely tried.

It takes humility to see the frailties and arrogance of others and still love them, and a willingness to put one's own

desires and needs aside in order to allow oneself how to be compassionate toward them.

Now, when life in the physical is easy, using these tools is also easy. So now is the time to learn. Just as a soldier learns to use his weapons best in time of peace, the soul learns to use its tools best in a time of ease and plenty.

There is more to the three pillars of the soul than actions in the physical world. They are relevant also in the world of the soul, but in a very different way. Nobody there needs a handout or a kind word, but they do need the equivalent in the form of energy. The young woman I saw, who was wearing her soul like Jacob's coat of many colors, was radiating energy. This is why my own soul left my body and moved toward her. It was elevated into a state of ecstasy by her soul energy.

Soul energy is expressed in those immortal colors Anne speaks about. Her soul is a deep and spacious blue. It's like looking into the top of the sky just at evening, at that darkening blue that seems like a window into eternity. Anne's particular vibrations—her colors—are unique to her and yet at the same time just as universal and immortal as all colors, and this is true of all souls.

But blue isn't her only color. She recently showed me her soul in three different colorations, red, green and blue. The red was her active side, the green her passive side, and the gorgeous, iridescent, glowing blue her soul in harmony. On this night, she came up beside the bed three times, each time wearing a robe of a different color. She was so vivid that I asked her if I could touch her hand. She gave me a worried look. Not that she was concerned about being touched. Maybe for an instant she even was material enough for that. She was worried because she knew that touching her would inflame me with desire and, when she had gone, leave me in an anguish of need and grief.

So, if we are soul blind and our egos are out of control, why are we even here? What's the point of placing ourselves in such a situation?

The reason is that physical life also a soul tool. It is, in fact, a soul-altering machine.

"When you know for certain that those of us without physical bodies are real and that we are with you, fear of death will end for you. Instead of hiding in your ego, you will move your attention into your soul. Then you will become able to practice soul craft, using physical acts and emotional states to enrich your soul colors."

"Unconditional love?"

"Objective love is craftsmanship, not sentiment."

Not all soul tools are entirely inner. Some of them are practical, external tools.

I had been inspired to do the sensing exercise by Joseph Stein and William Segal of the Gurdjieff Foundation, and had it explained to me by the head of the Work at that time, G. I. Gurdjieff's protégé Jeanne de Salzmann. I had understood it as healthy, practical work.

As my relationship with the visitors deepened, I came to understand that there was a basic grammar that I could use to relate to them, a sort of structure that would cause them to react in predictable ways, and therefore give me the opportunity to explore their motives for coming into contact with me more deeply.

They speak a very different language from us, and I don't mean words. I've never heard any words from them except a few in English here and there. However, there has been a rich communication in symbols. For example, the gray ones would often announce their presence by an appearance of owls, and if one goes into the habits and mythology of the owl, it soon becomes clear that, like them, the owl is a clever and silent night predator with eyes to see in the dark and ears so sensitive that he can hear little creatures scuttling in their burrows. His claws are powerful enough to dig right into the ground and pull out a little shrew or chipmunk. And indeed, the grays show up in bedrooms at the most improbable times and pluck us right out into the night. But the owl is also a symbol of wisdom with a rich history across many cultures, and to one who ceases to resist and tries to relate, much turns out to be on offer.

The most important thing they have to offer is this potential new relationship between the living and the dead, and it was, I am sure, because of them that I found myself, as I have mentioned, coming into contact with the people from between the worlds.

They came to meditate nightly with me, and when they announced themselves, it was the sensing exercise that they wanted to do. When I meditated by sensing my body, it seemed to give them a focus. Until the day Anne and I left the cabin forever, they worked with me to open myself inwardly—to let my mind be silent and my ego rest—so that we could come into the state of communion that enables the deep, rich inner search so necessary to building a strong soul.

So I knew that it was important, but it would take until after Anne died for me to discover that the sensing exercise turns the body into a sort of antenna that the nonphysical world can use to communicate with us.

It was in October of 2015 that I was shown why my wife needed me to do this.

I had decided to go to a William Henry event in Nashville, in part to be with treasured friends, in part to revisit the Scarrett Bennett Center where we'd held annual gatherings for fans of our radio show Dreamland, and in part because I was in such a very low, very lonely place in my life and I felt being there would bring me closer somehow to Anne.

During a break in the conference, a woman came up to me. She seemed quite nonplussed. Nervously, she said that she had something to tell me, but she wasn't at all sure how to go about it.

She began by asking me if I had a special chair, like a rocking chair or something along those lines. She then said, "I ask because I just heard Anne's voice in my ear. She said, 'Tell Whitley I can see him when he's in the chair.'"

At first I didn't understand. Then I did—and it was pure gold.

Given the state of my knees, when I do the sensing exercise and meditate, I sit in a chair and not cross-legged as I used to.

I realized at once that Anne could locate me when I was doing the sensing exercise and meditation. She could track me and come to me.

Once I realized this, my mind flashed back to an enigmatic incident that had taken place in 1988 or 1989. I'd had a brief dialog—mental or physical I cannot tell—with with one of the visitors, one of the few I've ever had. I asked why they had come here. The answer was, "We saw a glow."

At the time, I assumed that this meant the glow of cities, signs of intelligent life. But now, the moment the woman repeated Anne's words, I knew differently.

The real meaning was that when we place our attention on physical sensation there is an amplification of some kind that must give off a glow. That must have been what the visitors saw and why they came to me in the first place. They were curious about this one little glow that showed up night after night out there in the empty countryside.

I was excited. Had I finally found a means of communicating reliably with my wife, something that would work from my end of the bridge? Her ability to make people do things like make phone calls was by me unquestioned, but what about something more familiar, like conversation? Could we ever resume the wonderful journey in conversation that had been such a delightful and defining part of our marriage?

Naturally, as soon as I got home I went about meditating with redoubled effort. I would do the sensing exercise, then go deep into the quiet of my being, the place where the soul's whisper can be heard.

The visitors now reappeared in my life. They were here to help Anne.

CHAPTER 10

Know Thyself

IN THE DEAD of the night about two weeks after my return from Nashville, a series of shocks pulsing through my left second toe startled me awake. I jerked my foot and the pain stopped. But what had happened? It was three in the morning, dark and quiet in my bedroom.

I lay there thinking about the pain. It had been sharp, but now it was gone.

Could I have gout? I turned on my cellphone and searched for symptoms and no, this was not gout. It was more like an electrical shock. I examined the bed. There was no wiring anywhere near it. I don't own an electric blanket.

Mystified, I went back to sleep.

The next night, I was startled awake again. This time, my right nipple was pinched and pinched hard. This was much more painful than the shock, and I leaped to my feet.

There was nobody there, at least, nobody I could see. I looked at the clock. Again, three a.m.

I recalled back when I had meditated for months with the group of people from between lives. They would awaken me at three to meditate with them, usually by punching me on the shoulder. They'd also come back at dawn, and for a long time I joined them at eleven, three and six.

It occurred to me that doing the exercise at three, when most people were asleep, would mean that the little glow I generated would be easy to see. So maybe they were giving Anne some help.

I went into the living room, seated myself and began the sensing exercise, that simple matter of placing the attention on the sensation of the body, limb by limb, part by part until the whole body is included.

"I saw the glow," she says. "It worked. I got through to you."

"Why not just tell me."

"Because what we say sounds like your own thoughts. It wouldn't have seemed to you like objective information."

So I have been meditating at eleven and three ever since. For the first year, they would wake me up in various ways if I didn't do it. This could be quite startling, such as when something that felt like a small snake rushed up my nose, or when there would be a sudden, unexplained explosion. Later, I would hear a gentle call from the living room, "We're here." Now, they wait for me silently. If I fail on two nights in succession, they'll generally get me going again on the third night by blowing in my face.

Recently, for example, I simply could not rise from the bed. No matter how hard I tried, sleep would not release me. They made it quite clear that they were there, but I still just could not manage it. They let it go.

A few nights ago, I was again very tired, sleeping in a friend's country house. I wondered at three if I still needed to do it on vacation. A moment later, the doorbell rang. The house, however, has no doorbell.

Question answered.

I know that many people find stories like this unbelievable. But I am describing my life as I live it. In all my books, I have never done anything different. I have been truthful and accurate, always. I report with total honesty. I do this because mine is a life being lived in a new way—a life in contact with the nonphysical world, but absent the traditional trappings of belief and mythologizing.

It is extremely important to me to do both meditations every night, especially the three a.m. one.

"It gives me something to focus on. And I'm the one who blows on you. The best kiss I can manage."

"Now I want to not get up so you'll have to kiss me more!"

"Remember their sense of humor."

"So we're not alone in this?"

"Whitley, we are so not alone! We can't make much noise, so we really have to band together. Nonphysical consciousness in all its diverse multitude and size, can collectively manage

to project into the physical not much more than a sigh. The bridge is everything. When the bridge is built, the whole physical world will echo our song."

"The chorus of the angels?"

"If you want to say that, sure, but the song begins with you."

At first, I don't understand. Then I see in my mind's eye a dear old friend, Lorie Barnes. And with it, there comes another discovery.

When, after the publication of Communion, we began to get those thousands of letters and Anne took charge of the situation, she soon realized that one person simply was not enough, so she announced that she was hiring a secretary. I suggested a call to Manpower, but she said she'd find one among our correspondents. And indeed, not an hour later, she handed me a letter. "This woman will be my secretary," she said.

But when I read the letter, the author made reference not to secretarial work, but to singing and acting. When I pointed this out to Anne, she said, "Have you ever heard of her?" I said that I hadn't. "She'll turn out to be either a part time waitress or a secretary. Look at how well written this is, what a good hand. I think she'll be a secretary. Also, she lives two minutes from here."

She called her.

An hour later, Lorie, who was indeed an expert secretary, appeared at our door.

Together, they created a substantial file of letters, cataloging all of the ones that contained fulsome descriptions of experience. For years, the file was ignored. We created the Communion Foundation to finance its study, but could not get any grants.

Recently, Dr. Jeff Kripal, my co-author on Super Natural, became interested in the letters, and I donated them to his school, Rice University in Houston, where they will be archived for posterity and be made accessible to scholars.

They are a treasury of reactions to mankind's most extensive contact with another sort of reality and other intelligent species, physical and nonphysical both.

Many of the letters report encounters with gray beings with big eyes, some fewer with the squat, dark blue figures that have become central to my own experience, and beyond those with many, many other sorts of entity. Of them all, the dark blue figures, though, seem most concerned with our souls and our lives, and perhaps there is a very special reason for this.

The experience that prompted Lorie to read our book and write us a letter, in fact, involved these figures. It was the early fifties and she was pregnant. One night she was alone in her apartment in Queens. It was about 11 and her husband, a performer, was out on a job. She was reading in bed when she noticed movement and looked up. Standing beside the bed in a column were a number of short, dark blue figures.

In those days, there was no "alien" folklore save stories about beautiful Venusians and other tall tales along those lines. But Lorie found herself looking into the face of a bizarre, frog-like troll. As she recoiled in horror, it said, "Do not be afraid. We're not here for you. We're interested in the girl child you're carrying."

That only made it worse, of course. Seeing her terror, the figure added, "Why do you fear us?"

She said, "Because you're so ugly!"

Whereupon it laid a gloved hand on her wrist and said, "One day, my dear, you will look just like us."

It turned out that Lorie's baby was a girl, something that could not be known in those days prior to birth. She grew up to be a perfectly normal person, in no obvious way connected to any strange experiences.

Note this: they were not interested in her because of psychic ability or some other unusual trait. So why were they interested?

I suspect that they are interested in us all and involved with us in ways we are only just beginning to suspect. There is a reason that they told her that they were "soultechs."

The statement that was made, "One day, my dear, you will look just like us," is so strange that it suggests that we know even less than we imagine about what is really happening here, what our lives are and who we really are.

Maybe the human species has more than one form. It's not an uncommon situation in nature. Butterflies start out as caterpillars, for example. Tadpoles undergo an extreme transformation into frogs.

There is additional evidence that we may be more extensively involved with this other form, and that we may be filtering it out.

A psychologist was driving home one night along the Grand Central Parkway, passing LaGuardia Airport in New York City when he was horrified to see a huge jet dropping down onto the highway. His first thought that a plane had miscalculated the location of the runway and was going to crash into the dense stream of traffic. But as it passed over his car at low altitude, he saw that it appeared to be some sort of fake, that it wasn't a plane at all, but something that was designed to look like one.

The next thing he knew, he was observing an animated sign on the roadside. Strange symbols were passing across it. He saw a number of cars pulled over, and decided to satisfy his curiosity and pull over himself. Off the side of the road, he saw a group of people standing below the sign in a circle. Deciding to see if they knew anything about what was going on, he began walking toward them. Before he could get there, though, a shadowy sort of dwarf approached him. Blocking his way, it said "Get out of here." The tone was gruff and menacing, and he decided at once to comply. He got in his car and drove on—and that's where his story ends. He never found any explanation for what he saw.

Taking both of these stories together, a few things can at least be inferred. The first is that, whatever these creatures are, they are intimately involved with us. They are interested in our offspring. They gather groups of people together for unknown reasons, and protect these gatherings by utilizing distractions. They have told at least one person that, in the future, she will be one of them.

I see them all the time now. As of this writing, the last time I saw one was in June of 2017, and I'm sure that there will

be more encounters by the time the book appears.

When we had our upstate New York cabin, they would come there frequently. Once, when there were a number of people sleeping in our living room and two more in a private room in the basement below, they appeared. The people in the living room could talk to one another but could not move. What they saw were short, dark blue figures leaping around the room like acrobats.

Meanwhile, the couple in the basement were surprised to see appear at the foot of their bed the figure of a friend who had died in the Mexico City earthquake of 1983. She seemed perfectly solid, not in any way ghost-like. She said to them that she was all right, then disappeared. At about the same time, the figures upstairs also disappeared.

Later that month, I received a call from my literary agent telling me that there was a man desperate to speak to me, a person involved in aviation. Now, in those days, there were very many people trying to speak to me, but only this one had gone so far as to find my literary agency. I felt that I had to call him.

He said that, a short time before, he and his wife had been sitting in their living room at about ten at night. Their old dog, who was asleep on the hearth, unexpectedly became restless and needed to go out a second time. As the wife opened the front door to take him out, she saw what looked to her like a fireball crossing the sky and going down behind a nearby woods.

She called out to her husband, "I just saw a plane go in on fire. You'll get an emergency call in a few minutes."

At the same moment, their seven year old son came running downstairs saying that little men had brought his recently deceased older brother into his bedroom and he had said that he was all right.

The father was desperate to know if anybody else had ever reported such a thing, and I was able to tell him that they had—and that, in fact, Anne had discovered that the dead often appeared with the supposed aliens, especially these short, dark blue figures.

If close encounter truly involves aliens, then they must already be linked, their living and their dead. By bringing our dead with them during encounters, I think that they might well be seeking to help us become whole, too. But it may also be that what we are looking at is not an alien presence at all, but an aspect of our own species that mediates between the living and the dead.

The beings Lorie saw, the "soul techs," would, when they showed up at our cabin, often go into the childrens' rooms and shine lights on their bodies, saying that they were "doctors" and "looking at your soul."

Anne says they're "people who've done wrong trying to regain themselves by helping others."

I realize that they're the ones I called kobolds in the early days, dark blue, short. Human? That seems very strange to me.

"How are they helping?"

"One of the purposes of close encounters is to embed experiences like you and the close encounter witnesses have in your DNA. Future generations will be born with this record

in them. Because of this, they'll be able to take things farther. The huge increase in close encounters is about stepping up this process."

A soul tool is being used to make physical changes that will in future generations enable contact across the bridge.

"We will give you the most exact guidance that we can, but it won't be complete. It can't be because the future isn't nearly as well known to us as you would like to believe. The worst part is that, when we can't offer enough detail, people in contact with us will use their imaginations to connect the dots. That's what happens to psychics who give out wrong predictions."

"You've said some very exact things to me. The Trump election, for example." (She predicted in September of 2017 that Donald Trump would be elected president, something that at the time seemed completely impossible.)

"When I said it, it was definite."

"How can we know what questions to ask?"

"The best way I can think of is to ask about things that are not too far out in time. We can see the inevitable before you can, but not generally by much."

"Can all the dead see the future equally?"

"It depends on their focus. I'm focused on the physical world. On you. My whole life was preparation for being this kind of teacher. Not everybody is doing this, but everybody can be called to it."

"How do we do that?"

"Remember the love you felt for your parents, your

grandparents. Go back to it, the childhood love, innocent, trusting and so much a part of you that it flowed in your blood. It's very close to objective love. Reconnecting with it is what Jesus meant when he said we have to become as little children in order to enter the kingdom of heaven. Objective love is heaven."

One night in Malibu, in the spring of 2016, I began to find that out. I was at the home of friends, Leigh and Carla McCloskey, who often host speakers at their house. They have a large back garden, and on this evening a Tibetan lama was going to sit in it and chant. There were about fifty people there, some lying in the grass, others on chairs and benches. I was on a bench that looked across at a smaller bench that was unoccupied.

As soon as the monk started his repetitive prayer, I felt a change in my body. It wasn't unfamiliar. I have felt it many times during meditation. I would describe it as an increase in vibration, as if I was rising to a sort of higher speed.

In the next moment, I saw Anne sitting on the unoccupied bench. She was dressed in clothes she'd worn back in the 1970s, tan slacks, a green blouse and a sweater vest. It was an attractive outfit and I'd always admired how good she looked in it. Then she stood up and, without any sense of movement, I found myself at the bottom of a stairway. It wasn't a long stairway, but something like library stairs. I looked up and saw her again. She was looking down at me from at the top of the stairs. Behind her were rows of books. She made a little gesture, beckoning me to come to her.

But how could I ascend? I stood up anyway. Then I understood, because I could see my body behind me, still sitting on the bench. As I took one step and then another, the sound of the chanting died away. I entered a vivid, living silence and in a few steps stood before my wife. I looked directly into her eyes. There was a complete frankness there, a total openness. Also a sense that she was about to burst into laughter. And yet, had they not been so beautiful and so merry, the acuteness in her eyes would have made her frightening. Then I noticed her hair, which was full and beautiful. She'd always hated her hair, and one of our readers had sent me a letter some months before saying that she had told him that she had gotten better hair at last.

When that thought passed through my mind, she smiled. She was now full of laughter, brimming with it—at herself, at me, with herself and with me. It was comfortable, accepting laughter, but tinged with seriousness.

She took a green book down from the shelf and handed it to me. On it was embossed in thick gold letters the word "Life." It was the book, as I instinctively knew, of my life. I was rather nonplussed to see how thin it was. She gestured at me to open it.

When I did, I saw a young woman staring at me with a terrible expression in her eyes. For a moment, I was confused by this surprising image.

I had asked Anne to show me anything in my life that might explain why I am as I am. I know the literature of numinous experience well, which is why I know how alone I am in my life. Others have had strange experiences, many of them, but there are not many lives that are as consistently strange as mine.

I don't report most of these things. My criteria is simple: if there is some sort of corroboration, I will report an experience in detail. Otherwise, I keep them to myself.

I had been asking Anne to help me understand myself, and this moment was the result—the thin book, the young woman staring balefully at me.

My mother?

My birth was so hard that my mother had almost died of exhaustion. My head is big and it nearly killed her as I came down the birth canal. After I was born, I was unable to take her milk. I had to be fed on formula, and in the 1940s it did not provide satisfactory nutrition. I spent the first six months of my life screaming almost continuously.

I was so difficult to take care of that when I was six months old, my mother had to go to a rest home.

Back in 1988, I had an MRI scan, which I have described in various books. The scan is normal except for one thing. There are a number of bright foci on the surface of my brain. In 2014, I had another MRI, and the same marks are there.

Lesions like this are a characteristic outcome of battered child syndrome. Add to this the fact that two vertebrae in my neck are fused and the picture becomes tragically clear: at some point in my infancy, I was dropped on my head.

Did my mother do this? Is that what the message from Anne is about?

A group of doctors are interested in my brain. They know that I am no liar, and are examining my MRI scans. One thing is clear so far: there was babyhood head trauma.

Was my mother a child batterer, then? Is that why she was sent to the rest home?

I don't know and I will never know. There is nobody left alive from that time who might be able to tell me. I don't remember my mother as being a terrible woman. On the contrary, she was my best friend and most staunch defender and advocate. We had a dear companionship. I fondly remember our endless discussions of philosophy and literature, and how much an ally she was of her too-bright little boy. Once I showed up in grade school with Salinger's Catcher in the Rye. The nuns telephoned her about it. She told them, "He reads whatever he wants to read. That book came from my hand."

Was there a lapse when she was alone with her difficult baby and desperately tired? In late 1945 or early 1946 when this would have happened, my father was still in the army. She was taking care of me and my sister, then a toddler. She must have come home from the hospital still exhausted, only to discover that this new baby was in agony and was going to be basically doing nothing but screaming and sleeping, and that the doctors could not help.

If it happened as I think it did, then my heart fills with forgiveness. I say only that the mother who belongs to my memories and my heart is the one I cherish. I long ago embraced the message of the gospels regarding forgiveness, and also Anne's urging in "The Love that Led Me Home" to "put those burdens down." I refuse to cherish anger, even when it is justified, and in this case, I'm not at all sure that it is.

For one thing, perhaps I would never have lived this life without the injury. Head trauma is a characteristic of many people who display unusual psychic and psychological abilities. Obviously, I'm no exception.

So, on that night in Malibu, Anne started me on a journey into a truth about myself buried so deeply that I don't think I could ever otherwise have seen it. My mother, who loved me and who was the dear companion of my childhood, at one point in her life may have done me harm. This was the same mother, who, by the time I was eleven realized that my mind was hungry for much richer material than I could get from the children's literature of the time, and bought me the 54 volume set produced by the Encyclopedia Britannica called the Great Books of the Western World. She also introduced me to authors like H.H. Munro, "Saki", Franz Kafka, John Cheever, Thomas Mann and others. Salinger, of course.

In the Great Books, I found Plato's Dialogues, which excited me so much that I had to read them standing up. I would pace back and forth in my room, following the logic of the dialogues with intense excitement. The ideas and the way they emerged left me breathless. And Descartes—his work was so well designed, so careful and logical and yet so disciplined that I could not stop reading it. I just loved the way it made my mind feel, and I loved his famous presentation of Cartesian Doubt. Since then, I have lived a life in which I must practice this form of doubt constantly. He disciplined himself to doubt his senses. If I didn't doubt mine, my mind would descend into chaos. Keeping the question open is essential to my rationality and my sanity, and I have Descartes to thank for my understanding of how to do that.

I was alone as a child and am alone now. When Anne was alive, I had a real companion—she also had suffered abuse, she also had hungered as a child for great thought and found it in some of her father's books. She also was an advocate of the importance of drawing what we have lost in the unconscious to the surface in order to understand ourselves.

She used to say to me, "All you do is tell funny stories about your childhood. You need to face the truth." And now here she was communicating with me across the bridge between the worlds, helping me to bring to the surface contradictions and unacknowledged dreads that were burdening my soul, and would have continued as burdens after death if I had not been able to acknowledge them during this life, and include them in the love that is my core, and the core of all of us, the objective love that frees us from all burdens and grants us the lightness of being that we need to not only climb those library steps, but to keep going.

So now people can say of me, 'he got a bump on the head, that's why he imagines all this crazy stuff.' But I do not imagine it. I believe that the world as I see it is more accurate and true than the filtered version. It is possible for anybody to enter my world, too. You just need to know that it is here and that it is real, then learn how to notice its presence in your life. There is no need to suffer trauma.

When one begins to see the real world, the experience of being human becomes larger and more complex. Above all, the outlines of the bridge become more substantial, and those on the far side easier to see.

You realize that the real world is full of potentials and possibilities that we have tuned out, in fact, that nonphysical consciousness is much richer and more informed than we are. As you see this higher world, you also begin to experience this one as it really is, a sort of corner of something far greater than the physical could ever be.

As the scales fall from your eyes, you also see others as what they really are, every one of them.

They turn out not to be the small, pitiful creatures one might expect. Far from it. Ordinary people are vibrant expressions of something—call it a divinity—that itself seeks to be known and longs to be known but that cannot be known. And this anguished, joyous being, also, you can see as part of you and all of you, and as all.

Then, for the first time, you realize that you are looking across the bridge, and there in that form are all you have ever known or loved, ancestors, friends, departed lovers, and another is there, too, a strange figure standing a little alone, looking back at you with the same wonder you feel.

You realize that you are more than you thought yourself to be, because that figure, already on the far side of the bridge between life and death, is also you.

Thus comes the recognition that we live not only in our bodies but also on the shores of life. We are fishermen who cast our nets into the mysterious waters of our own beings. What we bring up is self knowledge, and that is the most powerful soul tool of them all.

CHAPTER 11

What Is the Soul?

I ASK Anne what she is now. She says, "We're light. Light, alive."

"Then why can't we see you?" She laughs. "I'm here!"

It's as if she's is just ahead of me, just along the road. "You say that the soul is light. What generates this light?"

"This is the energy of objective love, the desire to be itself. That's why people who approach it during near- death experiences describe it as enveloping love. It includes everything."

"But just calling yourself light isn't enough. When I turn on my reading lamp, that light isn't a soul."

"We're everywhere, but the light is undetectable."

"I saw you as colors, red, green and blue. Were you at those physical frequencies?"

"Those lower frequencies parallel the higher ones in our world."

"As above, so below?"

"This is why our world looks so much like yours. Why we look like memories of ourselves."

"What's the difference, then? Why are you above?"

"Remember the girl's dress. That was a very important teaching, Whitley. That's how reality looks from outside of time. How a life looks."

I want to ask more, but then I realize the value of what she has just told me. I have a taste now of the difference between above and below. We are inside the images the girl wore, moving through life as if along a path. In the higher world, we don't live our lives, we wear them. And that's what it means to rise above life on the wings of objective love. That's where she was.

I return to the colors. "Could an instrument have detected you when I was seeing you in the colored coats?"

"No, but the soul can be detected." "How?"

"Those orbs people record—not the dust and junk like that—the ones like were in our woods. Those are souls moving slow enough to be seen and detected."

"What do we need to do this more consistently." "Strong attention."

"So another tool of the soul?"

"Yes. You've cultivated your attention by doing the sensing exercise and meditating for fifty years. That's why you see what you do."

There is a tradition in human thought of relationship to this radiance that dates back to the earliest religious text we possess, and flows right through to the thought of American transcendentalists like Ralph Waldo Emerson, Henry David Thoreau and others.

When our world was simpler, it was easier to sense souls, both our own and those of the people around us, and those beyond physical life. This is because we were less distracted and so had moments of awakening such as the states of "transcendent wonder" described by the poet Tennyson.

Then, in the late 19th century we begin inventing technologies that, while wonderful, also had the effect of drawing us deeper into material reality. We created the telephone, the car, the plane, then the flood of devices that we possess now.

We forgot things like the light of transcendent wonder, and into the bargain we forget ourselves.

The first exploration of conscious light appears in the first religious document we possess, the Pyramid Text inscribed on the walls of the Pyramid of Unas in Egypt.

The record develops from there, appearing in every culture on Earth, fading away only recently. It has faded, but not died. In fact, it has been returning to our awareness. It is, of course, central to the stories of the near-death experiencers.

In seeking for an understanding of the soul, it's worthwhile taking a look at the history of the physical world's relationship with this living light, and to do that it's necessary to start at the beginning of religious thought.

The Pyramid Text is the first place in recorded human thought where the soul is represented as a serpent of light living in the spine— what some would call Kundalini energy and others the nerve pulses in the spinal cord. When, two thousand years after the Pyramid Text, Genesis was written, the soul was now seen as external to man, the source of his self knowledge. In the earlier text, it was seen as integral to being.

Neither vision is wrong. In fact, the vision in Genesis is an evolution of the earlier one insofar as it recognizes a separation between body and soul. It sees self-knowledge as self-will, thus indicating that man had reached another stage on the long journey toward the light— the glimmering girl I seek in my own life—which is the level of surrender, becoming as "a clear glass through which god can shine."

Later debasements of the Genesis text identify the soul as an evil being that is entirely separate from us—a demon who whispers the secret of self-knowledge to us, thus leading us away from union with god.

Certainly the demon rides—look at the world around us. When Anne was alive, she always said, "we are our own demons." Whenever somebody brought up demons and Satan, she would say, "Don't talk to me about demons. Talk to me about you."

In the Pyramid Text, the serpent is iahw, the light. It sleeps in the spine as the core life-force, the ta-ntr. It is circled by seven smaller serpents, nerve centers that became the chakras, or circles, of Tantra.

For it is in the Pyramid Text that Tantra is founded. In fact, it is in that text that the whole search toward the light began, Ann Sexton's "awful rowing toward God," Yeats's and my journey toward the glimmering girl and the search of those experts in the light, the Syriac and all mystics are seeking that which fades though the poet's "brightening air."

Brightening, though? It's not as if we were searching into darkness, then, and like all this wandering that has transpired since the text was written, it is into gradually increasing light. As the darkness falls around us, the light concentrates like the light of that man I saw on that night in the early nineties, brighter than diamond, calm in its eternity, sending out rays that, when they touched me penetrated my skin and left me with the taste of another person's essence, the naked truth of him, at once so precious and so common.

"I would like to feel you that way one day, Annie." "You keep going."

The colors of the chakras reflect the ascension of light from density to evanescence. The red of dawn is the deepest chakra, the dawn of the body. Next is the orange of morning, the wandering child, then the yellow of midday, then the rising light looking back at the green of earth, then entering and becoming the blue of the lower sky, ascending after to the indigo of the high sky, then the pale violet light of the Milky Way. Freedom, and I can feel it so clearly, that it is there even for me.

"Annie, are there beings in the stars who have already found the light?"

"It's not like that. It only looks like that from inside time."

"So is there a search, or has conscious energy already found where we're going?"

"Both."

The serpent in the spine is the road of ascension. In the Egyptian religion, it was the passage that the soul used to leave the body on death.

"What's it like to die?"

"You feel a shock down your spine. Something unlocking. Then you're lose. I flew out of the front of my body, not the top of my head. I shot out. Then I looked around and there you were with your hand on my chest. O my soul, I felt such strong feelings! I reconnected in an instant with everyone I have ever been and everything I have ever known. You looked so little all packed into your body. You're enclosed light. We're free light."

"What's that like? Do you disappear into something larger? 'Go into the light' as they say?"

"The second I was out, I felt an explosion of joy. I was out and there really was an afterlife! There was love all around me. I put my hand on you but you didn't notice. I showed you I could walk to make you feel better, and you saw that. Like I said, I was me. I still felt physical. I was still in the bedroom." "I saw you walking toward me, but I couldn't tell where you were. In a sort of neutral space was how it seemed."

"As far as I was concerned, I was in the bedroom with you."

"Did you go into light?"

"I am light."

Nestorius of Nonhadra in the eighth century describes this paradox very well, of being in light and being light at the same time: "You must give your attention to the simple light within you. In this simple light, moreover, a star will occasionally appear and shine, but later will hide itself and disappear: this is the mystery of the new world." He then describes an ascent in light that reads to me very like the ascent through the chakras first described in the Pyramid Text: "The light is the color of the sky, which is also the color of the nature of the purified soul. That color is the color of the firmament in which the intellectual insights of spiritual contemplation are situated like the stars."

When Anne showed herself to me in that deep, gorgeous blue, I felt the presence of a great purity. I can well understand it as "the color of the nature of the purified soul."

I ask her, "Are you a purified soul?"

"I am, but remember that life is a good alembic. The universe is full of purified souls. Don't put us on pedestals. Expect to join us."

Nestorius continues, "And when the light is that of

crystal, the very light of the Holy Trinity shines on the soul as well, and the light of the soul projects rays of fire which are the murmurings by which the soul glorifies God among the angels."

This is, I think, a description of the same rays I saw emanating from the soul I meditated with. They were living parts of him that conveyed his essential being into my own body. The beauty was fantastic—a direct experience, from my perspective, of limitless ecstasy. And that was just one small person!

"There's no such thing as a small person, Whitley. The glimmering girl you're following isn't just me. She's the final light of all knowledge."

"When you wanted me to start reading "Song of the Wandering Aengus," did you know why you were doing it?"

"My ego didn't but my soul did. My soul's been your teacher ever since the day we met."

"My soul's teacher?"

For an instant I feel—or perhaps remember—her hand on my hand.

I am so close to this light that it hurts, but I feel also that the fire of it is my own heart. Without being able to put it into words more articulate than these, I understand completely how it is that Anne can be all light and also herself, and how all are like this, even those of us locked away in these little time machines we call bodies.

The ancient Egyptian word for "life" and "snake" is the same word, hayy. It is the word both of the spine and the fiery serpent within it. It is this serpent of conscious light that ascends at death.

I first became aware of it in two ways. The first occurred in October of 1985 when I was being approached by the kobolds but not yet consciously aware of their presence in my life. I did not become aware of what had happened until March of 1986 when I was under hypnosis for the first time with Dr. Donald Klein. Unexpectedly, instead of going to the night of December 26, 1985, I returned in my mind to the previous October.

All summer, I had prowled the house in a state of terror,

protecting my family from the soft summer nights with a Benelli Riot Gun loaded with lead slugs. I had installed alarm systems. I'd sat outside my little son's room with the gun in my lap, then patrolled upstairs to check on Anne, then back again, over and over. Only when dawn came would I fall into a fitful sleep.

When Dr. Klein hypnotized me, I remembered seeing a short, dark blue figure standing in our bedroom. I vividly remember the shock that went through me during that hypnosis session, and the screams that pealed out of me. This fierce, terrible being approached me with a crystal wand, with which it struck my forehead. It elicited fearful images of destruction. Maybe they were actual, physical warnings, but I think it more likely that they represented the symbolic destruction of the world I had believed to be real. They were part of the process freeing my vision by unlocking my expectations.

But there was more to it than that. Also that October, I was experiencing extraordinary neck pain because of my then as yet undetected childhood injury. One night, it was so bothersome that I tried to twist my head with my hands to relieve it and maybe reduce the pain, something I had done many times before.

What happened this time was that another, unseen hand seemed to guide my movements. There was a series of what seemed like very deep chiropractic adjustments, in the middle of which there came a deep grinding sound and for an instant it felt as if my soul had fallen out of my body. The adjustments continued down to the center of my back.

I lay there amazed. For the first time since the pain had started when I was a kid, I felt complete relief. Wonderful. A weight that I had been bearing so long that I had forgotten that it was there had been lifted.

I had not only been freed of the pain, something in my spine had also been freed, and I became loose in my body.

After the Communion experience, I felt the close proximity of the figure who is depicted on the cover of the book, felt her presence much as I feel Anne's now. When I went into bookstores, of which there were many in those days, she would direct me to buy one book or another by saying in my mind, 'Get that one, open it to such and such a page,' that sort of thing.

One of those books was Robert Monroe's Journeys Out of the Body. Naturally, given who had directed me to it, I read it with avid interest. After I finished, I attempted an out-of-body movement using the method Monroe outlined.

I felt a loosening along my spine, then came rolling right out of my body and into the middle of our bedroom. I was completely conscious and normally aware. Of course, I cannot

know if all of my memories were intact, but I certainly felt like myself. I decided to go outside. After all, Monroe had traveled far and always gotten back. As a pressed through the slightly greater density of the wall, I reflected that this is how the visitors moved. They are souls, I think, that can assume a physical form.

Everything was covered with a thin film of shimmering blue light, even the ground and the electrical wires along the road. I decided to go no farther on this first try, but rather to return to my body. But when I tried to do that, its interior seemed to be covered with a slick, shiny film of what looked like mercury. I kept falling out and sliding down the bedside. I found that, if I just hovered, I slowly drifted downward. That worried me. I would rather have drifted upward.

The next thing I knew, I was in the front yard of my childhood home. My father was mowing the lawn. "When are you going to come help me," he asked.

I had hated mowing that lawn, and was instantly back in my body!

At the time, I thought that I would be able to get out again easily. But I never have, not that cleanly, not, in fact, until 2016 when the most amazing OBE of my life occurred.

I still did not understand the serpent very well, and the spine's function as the lock that keeps it in the body.

After Anne died, I wanted to go, too. I wanted to follow her and stay with her, and the more clear it became to me that she still existed and was a conscious being and still loved me, the more I wanted to go to her.

I attempted the Tibetan practice of p'howa, which is conscious release of the soul out the top of the head. I could not accomplish it, though, because my soul remained firmly locked inside my body.

Then, in the fall of 2016, I attended a conference at which there were a number of neurologists and professors who take an interest, as does my Super Natural co-author Jeff Kripal, in extreme human experience.

We were sleeping in dormitories with small private rooms and I mediated as usual at 11 and 3. Because of a long day of conferencing, it was particularly hard to get up for the three o'clock meditation, but I managed it. I collapsed back into the bed, looking forward to undisturbed sleep until dawn.

Instead, at 4 I felt a bolt of electricity shoot down my spine. I was furious. I had already done the wee-hours meditation. Why were the visitors waking me up again?

Exhausted through I was, I got up to meditate again. But it didn't work. I sat in the chair staring at the wall. Finally, I went back to bed.

Instantly, I shot out of my body and into the corridor. It was so sudden that for a moment I thought I'd made a mistake and stepped out of the room instead of turning to the bed. But when I tried to go back in, it was clear that I had no body.

My first thought was to try to appear to people. I am well aware of the fact that illusion of an OBE can be induced by applying an electrode to the right angular gyrus of the brain, which is part of the right parietal lobe and responsible for body image. Also of myriad efforts that have been made to explain the phenomenon away.

Anne says, "The first thing you realize when you leave life is that all of our beliefs are immature. We don't know enough to have beliefs."

Of course these academics and scientist would have the same knowledge of the brain that I did, and might well therefore assume that some sort of brain effect was responsible for my experience. So my first thought was to appear to one or more of them in the nonphysical state. Given that it's something that has happened to me a number of times, I had reason to hope that it would work.

I first tried the conference organizer, whose room was across the hall. I couldn't get him to wake up, though, and so went through the wall to the next room. Asleep, also. But in the third room I tried, the occupant was half awake. I lingered beside his bed until I saw his eyes open wide.

He describes his experience this way: "I was sleeping at around 4AM when I remember seeing you standing in the open area between the foot of my bed and the wall. Arms beside you, calmly looking at me as we talked telepathically for some time. I don't remember the topic but whatever it was, it kept me awake and was profound because I couldn't get back to sleep for an hour or two...You had on a one-inch colored checked shirt and you looked calm and happy but you weren't smiling. I guess I sensed you were calm and happy. You seemed to love me in some way because I felt comforted and calm when I went back to sleep. It seemed like a 20 minute talk and then you left through the ceiling."

I went so high that I could see the line of dawn crossing the continent. Above me were the sacred, silent stars, around me the indigo of the height of the sky. Then I raced down

across the continent, flashing through the dawn and onto what appeared to be a college campus. It was just after dawn, the sun was golden, the shadows were long.

The next thing I knew, I was in front of a building. Vision in this state is not the same as physical vision, at least not in my experience. For example, I don't generally see things that I did not know existed as what they are, but as something similar that is present in memory. If this is true for many or most of us, it must add to the disconnect between the physical and nonphysical sides of life. As time goes on and things change, the nonphysical side might well have less and less of an ability to understand what is happening in the physical.

"Which is why I didn't like you throwing out my socks. I need things to be the same there if I'm going to stay connected."

(The morning after she died, for some unknown reason I threw out Anne's playful mismatched socks, which were loud and fun and greatly enjoyed by her. I heard her say, 'you threw out my socks!' I bought new ones, and they are in her drawer to this day.)

In any case, I went into the dormitory. On the wall I saw a large black lozenge-shaped form. I have seen them before, but I don't know what they are. You do not see them when you're in the physical state. My guess is that they're creatures of some sort that exist in the level next to ours, which is perhaps material in some way that enables it to share our space without intersecting with it.

I wanted to see if I could enable anybody here to see me, so I went down the hall to the door of one of the rooms. Maybe somebody in the room would be awake. I'd seen a man of about twenty outside, but he had looked right through me. When people are motionless, like in bed or in a chair, it's easier to get them to notice you, I have found.

I saw what I took to be an exceptionally long dulcimer leaning against the wall outside the room. It had a fluted end, which made me think of a musical instrument.

There was nobody in the room, so I decided to go back to the conference. After all, I was halfway across the country. I did not want to lose track of my body.

I ascended once again and this time angled down the way I had come, and returned to my body easily.

Understand, I did not control this. Whoever sent that shock down my spine, unlocking my soul, was managing everything. And this is something that must be remembered about the whole OBE experience. We are not in control of it. Even when I leave my body on my own, where I go is controlled. That level of life is, I think, a conscious medium and being in it is being inside a greater mind, and being part of that mind. It is going to be deciding for itself who comes and goes and what they do and why.

At breakfast, there was quite a stir going. The man who had seen me had emailed a friend about it and people were talking about my OBE. I was delighted, frankly. I was there to describe unusual experiences, and I had provided one to this group who were studying them from a serious scientific and academic standpoints, not all of whom accepted the idea that they were actual experiences, but rather perceptions that seemed experiential.

Later that day, as I described what I had observed on the campus, it became clear that two of the professors knew the place I had visited: It was their university. They were even rather sure that they knew the specific dormitory I had visited.

In the spring of 2017, I went to the campus in physical reality. We drove around, looking here and there, until I saw a familiar building. It was indeed a dormitory. We stopped and went in, and I found myself standing in a place that I had never seen before except out of the body. Every detail was familiar, the placement of the furniture, all of it.

In wonder, I proceeded down the hallway to the dorm room. It was there, just as I had seen it. But leaning on the wall outside the door was not a big dulcimer but something that until that moment I had not known existed. This was a longboard, a type of extended skateboard. It had a fluted end, just as I had seen on it when out of my body.

I stood there reflecting on what was happening. The only reason this place was familiar to me was because I had been here while outside of my body. My soul had moved along this corridor while my body lay in a bed over a thousand miles away.

I bowed my head and prayed my thanks, and felt in that moment the truth of myself and the truth of us all.

I turn my mind back to the Pyramid of Unas and the authors of the Pyramid Texts. They had little in the way of material possessions. They knew hunger and pain and early death. Their understanding of the physical world and the nature of the body was deeply flawed and incomplete. But not the soul. This, they understood.

We are not used to engaging with the soul. We cannot see its colors or feel its presence in our bodies, along the spine to which it is attached or in the nervous system where it has its dwelling within us.

"Annie, what are we?"

"Light. Even the physical world, the body. All that is, is light. Slower or faster, in the end, it's light."

CHAPTER 12

The Most Powerful Soul Tool

WE UNDERSTAND how to build a house, how to write a poem, how to dream, but we don't understand how to think of ourselves as light. I look down at my hands, and I see physical objects. They feel solid. They're full of blood and muscle and bone, covered with skin. In short, they aren't light.

But then if I look a bit closer, I begin to see them differently. They are a complex of cells, each one an entity unto itself but none an island. My hands are colonies of cells divided into various different functional groups, all working together in sublime co-operation.

Looking even closer, I see atoms arrayed in intricate patterns, minute sparks of energy that are the actual building blocks of my hands. Closer yet, and the atoms lose focus. We imagine them as little planets with electrons orbiting them, but that's not what they are at all. Instead, atoms are fields of energy, nothing more or less.

So my hands look like hands and work like hands and are

constructed of physical matter, but, at the bottom, they are energy fields. Even deeper, they are a sort of memory. They are information. Data.

I am this data, a swirl of information suffused with light that is too energetic for us to measure, which we call the soul.

We are light.

The kobolds told Lorie Barnes that they were soultechs— soul technicians. They look at people by shining lights on them and into them. Something is reflected from within, inner light reacting to the outer light with which they are exploring.

Alfred Russel Wallace, who, along with Charles Darwin, discovered the principle of natural selection said, "Man is a duality, consisting of a organized spiritual form, evolved coincidentally and permeating the physical body, and having corresponding organs and development. Death is the separation of this duality, and effects no change in the spirit, morally or intellectually. Progressive evolution of the intellectual and moral nature is the destiny of individuals, the knowledge, attainments and experience of earth-life forming the basis of spirit-life."

Because he was a proponent of spiritualism, Wallace was a controversial figure in 19th Century scientific circles, exactly as he would be now. He was also, however, one of the great naturalists of the age and also one of the first advocates of the need to preserve the environment.

His description of the duality of body and soul fits very well both with my out of body experiences and Anne's NDE and her and many other descriptions of her entry into the afterlife. In fact, she described her experience of leaving her body in terms that mirror Wallace's concept quite exactly.

She says, "When I called you from my deathbed, it was because I was sort of falling out of my body. When you came rushing in, I was so glad. I thought, 'he can hear,' and I knew that we would stay together. When you put your hand on my heart and started saying goodbye, I just let go. I felt my heart stop. It didn't hurt. Then there was an unclasping along my spine. I popped out. I went right through your hand and into the air above the bed. I looked down at you with your head bowed and crying and saying goodbye. But why? I was right there, right with you. That was when I realized that there was an afterlife and I was in it and boy, that was exciting.

"I was me. I had on the clothes you saw me in. They were just there, part of the way I was imagining myself. Comfortable clothes. I felt like me, like my body but not sick and paralyzed and miserable. Normal. I felt normal."

For the kobolds, being a soultech involves examining the light body, but for us it involves using it.

When I am in the out-of-body state, I can often be seen by others in a recognizable form. One woman was horrified to see me standing in her bedroom in the middle of the night. She recognized me by the glasses I was wearing. In another case, a radio talk show host saw me in the night looking down at him from his bedside. He proceeded to ask me about it on the radio. The professor at the conference saw me standing before him.

Despite how I appear to others when I'm out, I don't perceive myself as a sort of lighter version of my body. I feel like a ball and I have vision all around myself. I don't feel borders like I do when I'm physical. I don't sense myself as light and I don't think I'm ever seen in that way. When I was on the college campus, there was a student walking toward me. I paused right in front of him, but he did not seem to notice me. And yet, the scientist at the conference certainly did, and recognized me immediately.

When we are alive, the light body is intermingled with the physical body. Generally when we die the physical body takes on an appearance of emptiness. It's movement stills, the light leaves the eyes. You can see death there.

But when Anne died, something rather different happened. There was a startling change in her appearance. I had been with people in their dying before, but I had never seen anything remotely like this. It was as if her features had not been composed of flesh and blood at all, but of some substance that surrounded her flesh and covered it. When she died this substance departed. What was left in the bed was a person with thick, straight eyebrows and narrow cheeks. She was shockingly smaller than she had been just seconds before.

It was as if some part of her that you could normally see had departed, leaving behind much less physical substance than is normal.

"I let go. It was easy. I was mainly concerned about you and A. My guys were really sad!" "More left than usually does."

"By then a lot of me was light. I'm big in light."

There is in Tibetan Buddhism the idea of the rainbow body. This is the body of a master, which, on his dying, leaves behind a group of signs. The first of these is a shrinking of the physical remains that occurs because so much of the body had already become light. Those of highest attainment are said to completely dissolve over a few days.

"I didn't."

"Did you see what happened to you in the hospital?"

"Pieces of me are still there."

"Would you donate your body again if you had it to do over?"

"Sure I would!"

Such a teacher, Annie! You're teaching me right now not to be identified with whom I love, because I'm having a hell of a time imagining parts of you floating in formaldehyde.

I can feel her laughing at me, darn it! "You died very pure."

"I did."

Another sign of the rainbow body is a fine mist that forms immediately after death. This is then followed by many rainbows.

When, in the hours after she died, I began to notice signs of the rainbow body, I did what I could to record them. I took a picture of the hearse disappearing into the mist that had formed upon her death. A few days later, I took more pictures of the rainbows that followed me to her wake.

"Were you a rainbow body?"

"Yeah."

"Is it different from going into the light?"

"Yeah."

"How?"

"I'm here in the living room talking to you."

"I can't see any special light."

"It's too fast for your eyes. I'm wishing it wasn't."

"I just think of somebody becoming a light body as grand."

"The man I saw like that was really magnificent."

"Not to him. To him he was ordinary. Like Dog. Dog is ordinary and magnificent both."

"When I'm meditating, I see you and Dog together a lot." "Yeah. Dog can be absolutely Dog and absolute at the same time."

The first really powerful manifestation of Anne's continued presence was the explosive event at the home of Trish and Rob MacGregor—a flash of light and an explosion.

"I had been going around trying to talk to people and nobody was noticing me. It was just plain odd and really annoying. You feel like yourself and you talk and nothing whatsoever happens. You yell. You completely forget about being dead, at least I did. I was racing around the country with no effort and not even thinking twice about it. When people would think about me, it was like a wind blowing me toward them and all of a sudden there I was with Trish MacGregor, who was sitting there writing about me. I said hello. No response. I touched her head. Nothing. Finally I just blew up. Then she sits up and yells and they both start running around their house. You would have loved it, Whitley, it was exactly like one of your practical jokes."

"So you weren't angry about your death?"

"Are you kidding? I was glad to get out of that hulk. But I was frustrated that everybody's so blind and deaf and—just plain thick."

I feel the past her frustration the sweetness and the other- directedness that keeps her here among us. I see that this mission that she is part of is why she lived and why she died.

These thoughts move me and cause me to feel her presence deeply. I feel as if I can almost see her light right now.

Now, if you look back over these paragraphs, you can, I hope, see something of the soul tool I am describing. It can't be put into so many words, this tool. At its core, it is a willingness to accept what we cannot see. The locked expectations of ego do not allow us to observe the way souls give of themselves. Ego always holds something back. If any words can sum up this soul tool, it is that it is a state of giving everything that one has to give—of giving one's light to others. In Anne's case, that light was symbolized by those rainbows.

If you want to start using this tool while still in the physical, you have to be willing to open your heart so completely that you will weep merely for the existence of others. You will be completely compassionate, but without ego, for ego will make you judge rather than see, and judging others has nothing to do with real compassion.

When the kobolds look into the light of souls, I suspect that they are looking for something like this compassion, seeking it by the way it shines. When they find it, I think they stay with that person, offering them support and teaching from inner reality, only rarely if ever emerging into the conscious surface of their lives.

My mind goes to some other ways of Tibetan Buddhism, most particularly the way imagination is used in its practice. One finds the energy of the deities in that theology by imagining their presence, and I see that the disciplined use of imagination is integral to the inner seeing that is so important to the proper use of this deep and elusive soul tool.

As we have gone more and more soul-blind, we in the west have ceased to understand this skill. Here we say, "just the imagination."

It is crucial, imagination, because of the empowerment it can bring. For example, you can imagine yourself to be completely compassionate and completely open. You can imagine that your ego is a tool, not a trap, and that you will not fall into judgment when you see your failings and the failings of others.

"You died pure. How?"

"Gave up my anger, mostly. I made a conscious choice: I would take the happiness road."

"But what about things like the Holocaust—mothers who died in

137

the gas chambers trying to protect their children. How could the leave happy?"

"Blessed are the persecuted, for theirs is the kingdom of heaven. Understand that you enter our world in the split of a second, often even before the body is dead. The people in the gas chambers were screaming in agony and terror, but they were also in the kingdom."

"And the murderers?"

"Forgotten."

"You've said something like that before. Forgotten in what way? Do they just disappear or what?"

"Souls too heavy to rise fall."

"They go somewhere, then?"

"You know."

Yes, I do know. I have seen that. I have been there. There were in my life two instances in which I was shown something relating to an underworld. The first occurred after one of the mediations with the people from between lives. They used to page through my mind, causing me to relive past events in startling and uncanny detail. One night, paging through my memories, they came across a moment during which I had been tempted to cheat on Anne.

They hesitated. Lingered. I writhed in discomfort.

After the meditation ended, I went as usual to bed.

I hadn't cheated. I'd only been tempted. So all was well— wasn't it?

In those days, I could not have told you what a soul tool was, but I was, on that night, being taught the deepest of lessons about this elusive tool. It is that the way to open one's own heart in true compassion is to give everything one has to the needs of others.

A few hours later, I woke up to see something so horrific that for a moment I simply did not understand what I was looking at. But then the two presences hanging from the ceiling above our bed became clear. But they were impossible. Nothing like that exists.

Except that they did.

I was looking up at two bulging black spiders, each easily two or three feet long. Their gleaming abdomens were ringed with yellow tiger stripes. I could see the pointed stingers at the base of their tails.

Worse, they were scrabbling against the ceiling, struggling not to fall on us.

Dear god in heaven, it had to be a nightmare.

I rolled out of bed, my initial impulse to run. But then I looked back and saw Anne lying there peacefully asleep. A few feet above her, the most unstable of the two looked ready to fall.

Now that I was on my feet, their appearance seemed entirely physical. I could even hear the rhythmic scraping of their claws as they struggled to find purchase against the ceiling.

I had never wanted so badly to run, never in my life.

But there lay Anne, completely helpless and right under them.

I stared at them. They were there. Impossible, but there.

I didn't see how I could attack them. They were far too big to crush. I thought of shooting them, but I dared not walk around to the other side of the bed and get the shotgun.

If there is such a thing as a demon, I was looking right at two demons.

And again, there was Anne. My darling wife, helpless, right there!

The scrabbling was louder. I noticed that one of them had built a sort of nest of spider web. Where they here to stay, then?

Then I realized what I had to do. No choice.

My only right move was to put myself between her and the danger by lying on top of her.

I stood there looking at them. They still appeared to be entirely real. The idea of getting even an inch closer to them was appalling. But I couldn't let them fall on her.

I told myself that they couldn't be real, but I also couldn't believe that they weren't.

I leaned down. There was maybe three feet of clearance between her and the one above her side of the bed. I was really close now, close enough to see the spiked hairs on its legs and the gently pulsating segments of its abdomen. In that moment, there was no way you could have convinced me that they weren't actual, physical creatures.

Then the thing shuddered. I looked up and saw one of its legs waving in the air.

I had to do it. Now.

I slid into the bed and lay on her. Her reaction— fantastically—was to sigh happily and open herself to me. But of course, she had no idea what was going on.

I was so scared that I felt myself getting dizzy. I was about to black out with terror, and here she was assuming that we were making love!

As completely as I could, I covered her with me.

I waited. Acid burned up into my throat. I shook like a leaf in a storm.

Nothing happened. I waited.

More nothing.

After a time, I noticed that the scrabbling of the claws was gone.

When I finally dared to turn and look, the ceiling was empty of spiders.

My wife was ready and we passed the deep night in the mystery of love.

I see now the depths of this remarkable soul tool, what it means to completely give oneself to the lives of others.

You do this and the part of you that is ego comes to seem small enough to contain. Because it would never, ever give itself so completely to another, you can see its borders. So this elusive soul tool is about discovering the borders of one's own ego by a process of completely selfless giving.

If I had failed the test and run, then things would have unfolded differently. How, I cannot know, but I do know this: nothing was going to prevent me from protecting Anne, whom I loved with all that I was and am. And I know also, now, another truth about me. Feelings at that level are objective. I would give myself in precisely the same way to anybody who came to me in such need.

Compassion sees only need. It forgets judgment and in so doing takes one out of ego and into soul.

The two things the visitors have been most intense about with me have been humility and protecting the hearts of others—in particular, Anne's heart.

A few years before, there had been not a test but a warning, and I will never forget it in all of my days and beyond my days.

In the years after Communion was published, Anne organized many groups to come up to our cabin. Often enough, as I have reported in previous books, they met the visitors.

Once, we had a group up which included a young woman who took a shine to me. She was attractive and I was tempted. I did nothing, however. Later, in Los Angeles, we once again encountered her and I was again tempted. Once again, I did nothing.

We spent that night in the Beverly Hills Hotel, and no sooner had I fallen asleep than I found myself being dragged downward through solid rock. I was in some sort of cage and I couldn't get out. This was more lucid than any lucid dream I could imagine. It felt real. As I shot downward, I realized that I was inside the legs of a gigantic spider. Nothing I did would release me. Those legs were like iron.

Finally, I managed to get out. I found myself back in my body, hammering my arm against the bedside table. The lamp was smashed, Anne was screaming—and I was shaking with terror.

I connected what had happened to the temptation the young woman had offered me, and resolved never, ever to even entertain such a notion again.

Souls too heavy to rise fall. I will never forget those words. But in these cases? A man is just vaguely tempted and he ends one time being scared out of his wits and another at the gates of hell?

There was, however, a reason.

Recently, I read the Science of Near Death Experiences, a group of papers edited by Dr. John C. Hagan III. In the paper "Distressing Near-Death Experiences: the Basics," by Nancy Evans Bush and Bruce Grayson, the case of a man who experienced a negative NDE after a cardiac arrest is discussed. He "felt himself falling into the depths of the Earth. At the bottom was a set of high, rusty gates, which he perceived as the gates of hell. Panic-stricken, he managed to scramble back up to daylight."

I know that panic very well. All too well. But I didn't do anything wrong! So why was I visited with these horrific experiences?

"If you had cheated on me and I had gotten mad and left you, our mission could never be completed. They feared for your soul, because you had no way of knowing then how serious the failure involved would have been. Only after death would you have seen it, and it would have crushed you."

"Would you have left me?"

"If you'd cheated once or twice? No. But if you'd made a habit of it, then our life together would have been ruined."

"This love is the most beautiful thing I can imagine. I never would have done anything to damage it."

I feel her drawing close to me once again. I find myself recalling a summer night, years after these two experiences were behind me.

We were living in Texas then, and we used to get up at two in the morning to walk because it was too hot during the day. We walked under the blowing trees. The south wind—the moon wind—was so swift and fresh that we could smell the sea a hundred miles away. On that night, I imagined that my soul and Anne's soul could become one. I wanted us to be one.

I remember as we walked along, I took her hand in mine. Her hand was warm and small in mine. I recall thinking that it was like the hand of the man from between lives, as light as air, a hand that was warm, alive and a shadow.

I kissed her fingers and she laughed a little, and the wind blew, and the moon flew in the clouds.

On that sweet night I sensed for the first time that not only were our bodies together, so were our souls.

Our bodies have parted but our souls never will. Had I cheated on Anne and ruined our marriage, we would not be here now. Anne's mission would have been destroyed because I would not have been here on this side of the bridge of love trying my best to record it and share it in this text.

So of course they over-reacted. They were terrified, and with good reason.

Fortunately, they scared the hell out of me, too. But for all that, what a great teaching. Give oneself to the needs of others and discover the borders of ego.

That, truly, is light. Enlightenment.

"You gave everything you had to this, even your life." "You, too, Whitty."

"I guess I did."

I feel her warmth against me, so close now. The kiss I couldn't feel —now I can. Souls can kiss, too, you know.

CHAPTER 13

Soul as Second Body

WE'RE TOLD that there's no such thing as second body, don't bother to look, nothing like that has ever been recorded or ever will be. So don't imagine for a moment that you have a soul, let alone that hungers for work and longs to understand and use soul tools, that wants to help itself and others, that loves all that it meets with encompassing objectivity.

Second body has been recorded. There's a photograph of it—one, single picture. It was left behind two thousand years ago, almost as if in anticipation of the eventual coming of an era when the soul would be generally dismissed and forgotten.

It is, if you will, an argument on behalf of the soul, left behind— with amazing insight—long before the debate had even begun.

It's been ruthlessly dismissed—debunked, as they now say. But that's a lie.

In 1977, Anne and I attended a meeting at which Father Peter Rinaldi was scheduled to speak about the Shroud of Turin. He showed images of the relic and spoke about the Shroud of Turin Research Project, which was then just being formed.

It was an impressive presentation, and we both found the positive images taken from the negative on the shroud to be perplexing. We contributed some money to the project and went on to continue to follow it over the years. The initial result appeared to show that it was indeed a piece of cloth from the first century AD, and that the image had been produced by a very brief, very intense burst of heat. But then in 1988 three separate laboratories carbon dated it to approximately 1260 to 1390.

We were disappointed, but also suspicious. By then I had been out of my body. I knew that the soul existed as I had been in the soul state. The first person to see me OBE had already reported her experience to me.

I had been trying to find friends and had ended up in her bedroom in the middle of the night. She lived in a city a thousand miles from New York and I did not appear to be entirely solid as I stood at the foot of the bed gazing at her. She was understandably furious and didn't talk to me for years. But the event had confirmed to me that the out-of-body state was real. So I knew for certain that what many people call subtle body or second body, or, as I do, soul, was, just like the physical body, part of nature.

I was studying it not through science but through the enormous literature of the soul and the work of the lively academic community that is devoted to it. Science may have retreated, but the academic world has not.

Later, when I met the people from between lives who meditated with me and saw that they could affect the physical world in a number of different ways, I understood that souls that are correctly prepared can still affect the physical. So I suspected that the man of the shroud, whoever he was, had been able to control his second body.

I knew, also, that the scientists involved in the carbon dating had for the most part started with the assumption that the shroud could not be evidence of soul life because such life did not and could not exist.

A few months before these results were announced, I saw just how powerful such denial can be in a mind that is not prepared to accept that there is more to reality than it believes.

We had a group of people at our cabin, among them a dear friend, Dr. John Gliedman, a psychologist who was also a physicist. He had seen enough at the cabin not to be completely skeptical about my experiences, but he was in complete denial when it came to the soul. He had been trained to believe facts and had fallen with the rest of the scientific community into the trap that only facts currently understood could exist.

The group of us went one morning to the clearing where I had originally been taken up by the visitors into their crowded little vehicle. As we were meditating together in a circle, a gorgeous beam of pure, clear light shone down from above. I was sitting in the center of the circle and felt it surround me with what I now understand from Anne's teaching was objective love. Of course at the time, I didn't understand. I could see the light around me and feel the love, but intellectually I was at a loss.

The others sitting around the circle all saw the light, all except Dr. Gliedman. He simply could not see it. About ten minutes after it stopped, the group of us went up to the cabin, excitedly discussing what had happened. We were in what I would describe as a state of joy. The light had been very beautiful, and had come with a wonderful, warm sense of love that felt remarkably compassionate and—well, just happy. It was happy light.

John continued to claim that he had seen nothing. I'm sure he was telling the truth, too. He soon had a debilitating headache. One of the members of the group, Dora Ruffner, was a body worker, and she spent the afternoon trying to help him with it.

I knew what that headache was about. In the months before I finally opened my mind to the close encounter experience and was able to remember what had happened to me in December of '85, I would have a headache just like it every afternoon. This was because I was pushing away what I was seeing at night. I could not admit it into my reality, not without seeing my whole view of the world collapse into chaos.

It is that fear of chaos—the mind unmoored—that drives all of the denial that curtains off reality. We live in the world as it appears, not as it is. In other words, we live by assumptions. We cling to them, desperate not to fall into the reality of mysteries and questions in which we actually live.

Dr. Gliedman was in the same predicament. Something had appeared in his experience that was outside of what he believed to be possible. Many people, not just scientists, would have had the same experience he did, I feel sure. We cling to a limited world view for many different reasons, and only patient inner work over time can pry us lose from it.

"It's locked expectations. They narrow the slit through which you view the world even more than nature does. Unlocking them takes patience, self-respect and an openness to new possibilities. Look into the eyes of an infant. There you see unlocked expectations. Go as far back as you can into your own childhood, remember how it felt then to be alive. That's how to start opening your expectations. To be truly awake is to have none."

Clinging like John and I did to our locked expectations, the scientists who did the carbon dating could not allow it to show the actual age of the cloth. No matter how objective they believed themselves to be, in fact they could not have been.

And indeed, it has since developed that some of the fragments of material that were removed from the shroud for the experiment may have been part of a repair that had been made at a later time, although admittedly not all. But the fact that the cloth was in a fire could throw off carbon dating. This, however, was not taken into account.

Subsequently, more and more evidence has accumulated that the shroud is indeed from the Roman period. In 2009, Barbara Frale, a paleographer at the Vatican Archive, imaged the shroud and found writing on it identifying it as the burial cloth of "Jesu Nazarene," a description that would not have been used in the middle ages as it would then have been heretical not to identify him as Christ. His Roman executioners would have labeled his shroud in this way.

In 2015, geneticists at the University of Padua analyzed DNA on the shroud, determining that the most abundant human DNA present came from Druze people, meaning that it was probably in the middle east for an extended period of time. But there is no way to account for this if it was a 14th Century forgery. Also, the oldest DNA found on it came from India, not Europe where the forgery is supposed to have taken place.

The herringbone weave of the material would have been extremely rare in 1st century Jerusalem, something reserved for only the most luxurious cloths. It would have been even more so in 14th century Europe. Only one sample of similarly woven linen has ever been found from the medieval period.

This is an important finding, because it means that the cloth on which the image appears would have literally cost a fortune. But what forger would spend that on something intended to make a profit in the thriving relic markets of the 13th and 14th centuries?

It would also have been an extremely valuable item in the Jerusalem of the first century, something that would have been used in the burial only of a person of high stature, and affordable only to an elite few—like, for example, Joseph of Arimathea. Another burial shroud has been recovered from a first century tomb near Jerusalem. It is definitively carbon dated to the first century CE. It is layered together, not woven, and is made of wool and linen, not pure linen.

In 2017, it was announced that the red marks on the shroud are human blood, and not only that, but that the blood was from a person who had been stressed, probably by torture.

In a peer-reviewed paper entitled, "Atomic resolution studies detect new biologic evidences on the Turin Shroud" published in Plos One by Elvio Carlino, Cinzia Gianinni and Giulio Fanti of the Institute of Crystallography in Bari, the authors write, "we used atomic resolution Transmission Electron Microscopy and Wide Angle X-ray Scanning Microscopy experiments studying for the first time the nanoscale properties of a pristine fiber taken from the

Turin Shroud. We found evidence of biologic nanoparticles of crea-tinine bounded with small nanoparticles of iron oxide. The kind, size and distribution of the iron oxide nanoparticles cannot be dye for painting but are ferrihydrate cores of ferritin. The consistent bond of ferritin iron to creatinine occurs in the human organism in case of a severe polytrauma. Our results point out that at the nanoscale a scenario of violence is recorded in the funeral fabric and suggest an explanation for some contradictory results so far published."

Thus the previously published claims that the markings are paint appear not to be correct, based on this more sophisticated test.

While there still isn't conclusive proof that the Shroud is of middle eastern origin or that it was created during the first century AD, or that the man of the shroud is a Nazarene called Jesus, there is now a significant amount of evidence that all of these things are true.

There have been many efforts to duplicate the image on the shroud, and some of them appear at first to be convincing. However, all efforts to use a camera obscura such as might have been available in the middle ages leave an image on the linen that is much deeper than the one on the shroud. Physicist Paolo di Lazzaro of Italy's National Agency for New Technologies, Energy and Sustainable Economic Development, an expert on the Shroud, explains the prob-lem: "the color's penetration into the fabric is extremely thin, less than 0.7 micrometers (0.000028 inches), one-thirtieth the diameter of an individual fiber in a single 200-fiber linen thread." He went on to tell the National Geographic in 2015 that the ultraviolet light that would be necessary to create the shroud image "exceeds the maximum power released by all ultraviolet light sources available today." In addition, "pulses having durations shorter than one forty- billionth of a second, and intensities on the order of several billion watts," would be necessary.

No energy release like this is possible now, nor has it ever been possible. And yet the Shroud of Turin exists.

A flash of energy—light—of extraordinary intensity and extreme brevity caused the image to appear. What the effect, if any, of such an event might have been on the rate of carbon decay in the cloth is unknown.

So the shroud remains a question on two levels. First, there is the carbon dating that suggests a medieval origin. Second, there is the impossible nature of the image and the fact that it cannot be duplicated without causing a much deeper burn than is, in fact, present on the cloth. And then there is that remarkable flash of light.

I have seen beings of light with my own eyes. I have been suffused in it and sometimes during deep meditation seen it inside my own body. I know this light, although not, obviously, at the intensity that created the image on the shroud. I think that this light is subtle body, second body or soul. It is in a larger sense, being. And, as Annie has said, "God is the community of being."

If we look to what was seen after the resurrection of Jesus, what we find is the emergence of a second body of breathtaking power—in fact, the most powerful manifestation of the soul ever recorded in the history of this species.

Anne was a scholar of the gospels, and one of our most frequent discussions involved whether or not the resurrection happened. We explored the idea that Jesus might have had a twin, which is part of the very ancient tradition of the Syriac Church, for example. But if he did, why were the apostles surprised to see him after his death? They would have simply assumed that this was the twin. And surely, in that small world, the existence of this twin would have been known. During Jesus' lifetime, there would have been no reason to keep him secret, and certainly, after Jesus was executed, the last thing a twin would have wanted to do would have been to start walking the streets.

The reasons that the Romans executed Jesus were two. First, he was openly claiming to be the Jewish king, in direct opposition to their own puppet king, Herod. As a Nazarene, he would have been considered a descendant of David and thus a far more legitimate claimant than Herod. Second, when he attacked the money changers, he threatened the flow of money into the temple and thus the whole financial edifice on which the stability of this new Roman province depended.

He was a political rebel and he was killed for that reason, but only after he appeared in Jerusalem. The Romans didn't care what he did in Galilee. They knew that the Galileans would never follow him. This was because, just a few years before his birth, there had been an uprising in the area and the central Galilean city, Sepphoris, had been sacked by the Romans and its citizens either sold into slavery or crucified by the thousands in the surrounding hills.

The Galileans heard only the political side of his message, not the subtle, stirring moral message.

All four gospel accounts of the resurrection mention that beings of light being were present in the tomb when the two Marys went to anoint Jesus's body. John says that there were two of them, dressed in white. Matthew describes a single being, his appearance like "lightning." Mark describes his clothing as "lightning white." All four gospels agree that he was dressed in white.

As I have said, I have seen somebody who could easily have been described as "lightning" at one point. When he was in physical form, the tunic he wore was white. So, as far as I'm concerned, such beings are as real as we are.

The one I saw in physical form was careful not to move, I think because he was concentrating very hard in order to appear as a material being. But Jesus walked with his followers. At one point he even ate with them and, of course, placed the hand of Thomas the Twin into his wounds. Anne always maintained that this was his twin brother, and he appeared with Thomas to prove that he was not the same person. And then we would wonder if he really even died on the cross?

She was certainly very good at enjoying the question, and I recall those conversations with fondness and longing.

If, as it would appear, what came out of that tomb was

Jesus's second body still in coherent form, he must have had a very powerful attention and a fantastic ability to sense himself in order to manifest so clearly to people. It is my belief that it takes two things to accomplish this depth of soul-sensation: lightness of being and strength of attention. The man I saw do it could never, I don't think, have walked around a room. I doubt that he could even have spoken, and, given how rarely it is done, he must have been a real master of the skill.

Jesus was very extraordinary, but at the same time, judging from the deplorable condition of the poor fellow who left his image on the shroud, very much what he said he was, a "son of man" who had been treated with great cruelty by the Romans.

To assert that the resurrection really happened, and I think that it did, is not to also say that the tenets of Christianity as they emerged in the centuries following the event must be followed to the letter. On the contrary, to understand his message it is probably best to go to documents like the Gospel of Q, which is a compendium of consistent statements from the gospels that scholars believe represents an earlier document from which they were all derived.

"It's all about light, Whitley. Letting the light enter you. But you have to have a loving heart, show compassion and be humble enough to open yourself to it."

"It feels a bit like disappearing."

"Ego does disappear. It doesn't end, but it steps aside to let the soul take the attention. That's what it means to become as a clear glass through which God can shine."

So we have been set quite a challenge by this man who lived and suffered and died among us so long ago. But now, as

we come to the time when Earth's womb is no longer able to contain us, we need to revisit that message in a new way, with pure hearts and in true humility.

It's evening now, a warm summer night, and I remember back across the river of evenings I spent with her. When our work was done, we would make our supper and converse together. Such precious times, and I feel her now as I did then, her rich conversation and her humor.

She used to say, "People are too ominous about the gospels. Jesus had a great sense of humor. He accepted that people fail, and he forgave."

She used to laugh about Mary Magdalene at the tomb as her visit is described in John, thinking that Jesus was the gardener.

The green man was a fertility god in much of Europe, replaced by Jesus as the resurrected one. Anne often wore green to public events and encouraged people who came to see us to do the same. She said it was the color of those who loved life. She used to say, "I'm a resurrectionist. That makes me a green Christian." She meant that Christ is identified with the old pagan Green Man all over Europe. The resurrected Jesus is the pagan god of fertility in a new form, not as the rebirth of plants and the things of the earth, but as the rebirth of the soul.

When we realized that the shroud really did tell the story of the resurrection, it changed us both profoundly. It freed Anne and delighted her. She would say, "the resurrection didn't just happen at a certain time. It happened outside of time. It's always happening. You can feel it."

I couldn't. I guess it's my Catholic upbringing, but I worried too much about sin to really embrace something as wondrous as that.

"The worst curse that was visited on Jesus after he left this world was the one that claims that he was in some way special, apart from us, a deity separate. When they started calling him Christ, that was the darkness within us trying to put out his light. He was just a guy, Whitley, who had surrendered completely to the light. That's why it shone through him so brightly."

"I still worry. I worry about being sinful." "Let's talk about it."

"How it weighs us down—that's what I worry about." "We don't see sin that way at all. Here, it looks like disease." "That's—surprising. I've never heard that before."

"Sin seen objectively looks like sores." That stops me. A memory tries to surface.

Then I realize what it is and I'm shocked. Moved. I haven't thought about this in years, and now here it is come to mind again, this time with the power of revelation.

Back in the 1980s I had a very striking dream—what's called a lucid dream. In it, I was walking along a road in a pleasant area of low shrubs and brush. It was about midday. As I walked, I noticed some movement in the brush. The dream was so vivid that I was as wary as I would have been in real life. As is often the case, I had the sense that I was not exactly dreaming, but also that this was not exactly the real world, at least, not our real world.

Out into the road came a man, naked and filthy. My immediate reaction was to try to help him. However, as I looked at him I realized that he was covered from head to foot with livid, running sores.

I couldn't imagine how I could help somebody in a state like that, and I didn't want his infection to contaminate me. I stepped back, moving away from him. He came toward me, reaching out to me. But he was slow, barely able to move because of the encrustation of scabs and infection that covered him.

I woke up. It was still dark. I sat up in bed. I was covered with sweat. For a moment, I thought that I was going to vomit, but the sensation passed. I went into the bathroom and got a glass of water, then went back to bed.

For nearly forty years now, that dream has lingered in the back of my mind. I sensed that it was important but didn't know why.

About fifteen years later, I saw him again. He was better, many of the sores healing.

"He was giving up his regrets." "His sins?"

"Evil acts here are remembered only in regret. His soul was sick with it."

"Then if he'd just forgotten about his sins, he would have been fine? No consequences?"

"You can't forget a single second of your life. Not anything. No filters here, no pretending."

"If he can't forget, does that mean the sores are there forever?"

"Remember 'put those burdens down?' Easier to do that when you're still in the physical, which he could have done but didn't. The brain is a wonderful instrument. It can cause soul infection, but it can also heal it."

"We think in terms of good and evil."

"That's a level of emotion that stays with the physical. We see sick souls, not evil people."

"No punishment?"

"Do you think he wasn't punished?"

"God gave him the sores, then?"

"His life gave him his regrets and only he can reconcile them. Nobody can cure us but ourselves. There are no miracles here."

Once again, no miracles, just nature. It is so important to remember that the world of the soul and conscious light is a natural world. It is like everything else, part of nature and subject to the laws of nature.

In that sense, the resurrection was a natural event—the light bursting out through a man who had surrendered himself to it entirely. So also, the man covered with sores—he was part of conscious light, too, and so also part of nature.

Both of them—the first and the last—were part of the same aim, the journey into ecstasy that is the reason that everything exists and why those of us who have been given the gift of intelligence are so precious. Everything that is, is on the journey, but those of us with knowledge of life and death and the life beyond, we know it.

That's why he died for us. Because we know and are alone in what we know of death, and doubt the world beyond.

The greatest act of compassion ever seen on this earth was not Jesus letting himself die on the cross, it was what came after, which was the revelation that second body—the soul—is real. It was the resurrection.

CHAPTER 14

A Hidden Plan?

STARS EXPLODE. Devouring black holes wander the firmament. Asteroids and comets strike planets. Stars, even whole galaxies, collide. Vast cycles rule life on Earth, cycles far too powerful for any human intervention ever to change. And all of it seems to be random.

It isn't all destructiveness, though. Our planet is precisely the right amount of distance from the sun to enable life to form. The moon is exactly large enough and precisely close enough to put just the right amount of drag on the planet's rotational wind to slow it down enough to enable complex creatures to evolve. The planet is shielded from strikes from cosmic debris by the gravity fields of the gas giants in the outer solar system and by the closeness of the moon. Jupiter and Saturn will take the first hits and if anything gets closer, the moon will work as a shield. The result of this is that large asteroid strikes are much rarer on Earth than they are on the other planets. Earth isn't pockmarked with craters because the moon is.

Looking at the precision of all this, it's easy to think of the Earth-

Moon system as something designed, a life building machine carefully constructed to shield its inhabitants from as much of the random destructiveness of the cosmos as possible.

Is there a mind behind it, then? Or is it simply that the universe is so huge that this spectacularly improbable situation was inevitable, and we are the children not of consciousness but chance?

There are strong arguments for randomness, but it is also true that a strangely high level of what looks like good luck is needed to explain why things have developed as they have.

I hesitate to join the heavily politicized intelligent design argument. Even if design is part of the picture, there is no reason to take a step farther and claim that a biblical god, ancient aliens, or some other known or imagined factor is responsible. If it's true, something must be responsible but what remains an open question.

So, is there a presence subtly shaping and forming the world—shaping and forming us, also?

If the universe is not a motiveless, random system governed by chance and statistics, then it might be a living thing that has motives and expectations, and, one might suspect, dreams.

For example, there is something eerie about the cycles of expansion and extinction that have characterized the evolution of life on Earth, including both our physical evolution and the evolution of human culture.

Our cultures haven't just been affected by some distant creating hand, they have been repeatedly upended by what I call incidents of light—instants of intervention, each lasting only a few seconds, that have changed everything.

Moses saw such light in the form of a burning bush and we ended up with an entirely new concept of God. In antiquity, every temple in the world contained a statue of its god. The statue was believed not only to exemplify the god, but to contain it.

The god of Moses was radically different. The holy of holies in the temple in Jerusalem was empty because, following his god's instructions, Moses had told the Jews that he had no form.

This remarkable change effectively made this god immortal. As he cannot be seen he cannot be finally identified and understood, which is why he has remained relevant for so long. His nature evolves with our idea of him, which can never be fixed into any specific form. By contrast, Ra lies in ruins in the Egyptian sands, Athena is lost from her Parthenon, and the Temple of Jupiter Greatest and Best in Rome is a tumble of columns.

But "God"—our God—who came to Moses as a life changing and mind changing burst of light, is with us still, to this day challenging us to seek deeper and see more.

When, after his resurrection, Jesus ascended, he was surrounded by this light and absorbed into it.

Whatever precisely happened, it was so powerful that it sent a group of poor men and women out into a hostile and dangerous world to tell about it. They did this by walking from city to city, entering the marketplaces, raising their voices and speaking out. They did it in a hostile community without anybody to defend them and they accepted their lonely deaths on its behalf.

This light has power.

Paul the Apostle saw a flash of it on the road to Damascus and was so inspired that he changed from a persecutor of the followers of Jesus to a disciple of his teaching, and also went out alone into the world to spread his word. Christianity was thus born out of a flash of conscious light.

Mohammed saw it in the form of an archangel in a cave, and the Qu'ran came to be written. He, also, took his message into a hostile world and found himself having to do battle for it, and almost lost everything as a result. His inspiration was so powerful, though, that it transcended all resistance and caused another religion to appear. But like them all, its pristine brilliance was quickly distorted by those who seek power over others, and now it is hardly a shadow of what its creator and his vision must have intended.

Mohammed never for a moment countenanced anything remotely like strapping bombs to children and using them as murder tools. As well, you have the religion created out of the words of humble Jesus identified with vast cathedrals and immense wealth, and a fifteen hundred year long history of oppression.

These and other incidents of light have injected very pure ideas into our world, but so far we have not been able to handle their energy, and have consistently turned them into cruel and confused systems of belief that have nothing to do with strengthening souls or making the physical and nonphysical sides of our species into a coherent whole. They also don't address the larger question of why they happen.

Science can speculate. So can religion. But it's only speculation. Science cannot prove that they were all misapprehensions any more than religion can prove that they represent interventions by deities.

Nevertheless, there is something happening here on a very large scale that does suggest design and intention. In some ways it cradles and protects life, but it also has a habit of upending everything with truly exceptional violence.

Or maybe the destruction is random, and the strange way the planet generally recovers is what is designed.

For example, Earth is changing once again right now.

But to understand this, it's necessary to first explore her more distant past.

Earth has seen many different geologic eras, each one peopled by its own unique array of species. It has gone through at least five major extinction events that destroyed the majority of the species then alive.

So, was this chance or not? Or some chance and some design? And, above all, what does it mean for us right now?

I ask Anne if she knows. "Not at all."

"You don't have perfect vision of the past?"

"I have perfect vision of this past life and a sense of others stretching back—a flavor of me that is my essential identity. But as to the dinosaur era and so forth, I didn't exist then."

"So we're not there from the first. What brings us into existence?"

"A species is an idea. We are all part of the great idea that is man."

I think again of the sentence from Physics from Fisher Information that she left behind, that the universe began as "a single, primordial quest for knowledge." I can well imagine something seeking, questing and questioning, coming up with ideas, experimenting, wiping the slate clean and trying again, on and on.

"We can know the stories of our own souls, but not those distant histories. You don't die into a state of total knowledge. You die into the knowledge that you bring with you."

I have made it my business to search through the deep past for the fingerprints of the designer. If there is a deep plan, it is hopefully possible to at least see its outline.

As, indeed, we can.

When the planet was just forming, something so enormous hit it that the crater it left behind is now known as the Pacific Ocean. What remains of that strike is the moon.

If the moon was not here and in a close orbit, there would be no higher life forms on earth. This is not only because it protects us from asteroid and comet strikes, but also because its gravity retards what would otherwise be continuous orbital winds blowing with hurricane force. Nothing more than lichens could grow on a surface scoured like that.

So the collision that created the moon was the fundamental shock on which everything that has happened since depends, right down to the loves and hopes in the shadows of your mind, and your children at play there in the back garden.

Was it an accident, then? When you add it to all the other things that life and evolution have depended on—the location of the moon near the earth, the placement of the outer planets in just the right position to absorb the impacts of incoming debris, the fact that the sun, unlike most yellow dwarf stars, is strikingly free of the huge solar explosions that regularly sterilize their planets with radiation—you have to wonder if you are not looking at a gigantic design. Not only that, we do not see the gamma ray bursts coming from the center of our galaxy that are present in most of them, and which render them permanently sterile.

So a benign star in a benign galaxy, a planet the perfect distance from its star and a moon in exquisite orbital balance with it are what have enabled life to arise and evolve here.

If somebody desired this—desired life—in the stretching vastness of the desert that is this universe, they might only be able to fulfill that desire by creating a place like this. And if they were, further, interested in deepening its perceptual experience—perhaps so they could look through its eyes like a child peering through a magnifying glass—they might use evolution to create ever more sensitive creatures, from the earliest microbes all the way to man.

But the exquisitely protective crucible we live in is not the only factor that enables evolution. Sometimes things are changed. The blackboard is erased. Life is put under ferocious pressure and forced to either adapt or die.

"That I understand. It happens in individual lives, too— not just physical lives but the long, evolving lives of souls. The evolution of the individual parallels the evolution of the species, and that of every species the evolution of the whole. Evolution is holographic."

"You say you don't know anything about the deep past, but I see great insight in those words."

"We know only the facts we bring with us, but all the principles we can understand."

So we'll go back, then, and see if a very large scale picture can be at least glimpsed. Maybe something of the designer's mind and motives will be revealed.

Multicellular life forms emerged about 580 million years ago, and since then have been getting steadily more complex, more sensitive to the world around them and, perhaps most important of all, more curious. Compared to the basic perceptions of a bacterium—nutrition, need, light, dark—the perceptions of a human being are as a whole universe is to a single grain of sand.

As Anne said, if people haven't led rich, searching lives they can be very minimal when they die. But they can also be, I would think, towering miracles of consciousness.

And yet it's not safe here. For all the protection that surrounds Earth, it really isn't safe here at all.

Something like 99% of all species that have ever existed are now extinct, and there have been five great mass extinctions.

The third one, the Permian mass extinction which happened 248 million years ago, killed 96% of all species then alive. Everything living now, including us, is descended from the 4% that survived. The most famous extinction is the fifth, the Cretaceous mass extinction, which killed off the dinosaurs.

Right now, we are in the midst of a 6th mass extinction. The stage for it was set when the current ice epoch began. This is called the Quaternary Glaciation, which started 2.8 million years ago. During this period, the ice has expanded and retreated many times, with each ice age lasting about 100,000 years. They are punctuated by inter-glacials, and we are at the end of one of these right now.

In geologic time, these are very brief events. Looked at from the perspective of hundreds of millions of years, it's as if Earth is currently having a sort of seizure.

The extreme climate cycle that has characterized the Quaternary has caused a lot of species migration north and south as the planet heated and cooled, but also a steady process of minor extinctions.

15,000 years ago, that process intensified with the end of the ice age, the destruction of the mammoths and many other species, and has now accelerated to a scale and speed not seen since the extinction of the dinosaurs.

This is happening because the constant cycling back and forth between ice ages and warm interglacials is keeping habitats in constant flux, and now human activity is pouring greenhouse gases into the atmosphere, functioning like a continuously erupting volcano.

Most of Earth's geologic history presents a very much more benign picture, with epochs-long periods of stability and slow change. Violent events such as mass extinctions are rare. However, while the wildly variable climate cycle we are in now has caused some extinctions, it has also forced much more rapid evolution on adaptable species, the chief one of which is man.

"When physical intelligence reached a certain level, consciousness realized that it could not only be aware of itself, it could contemplate its own meaning. Across the universe this has happened many times and consciousness looks at itself now in billions of different ways, through the eyes of countless minds. Still more minds are desired, which is what led to the current epoch here on Earth. The stress brought on by the continuous changes in climate of the current period are intended to speed up evolution on Earth."

Homo Habilis, the ancestor of the whole human line, appeared at the same time that the Quaternary's stress-inducing ice cycle began.

Did Homo Habilis possess some version of "I am," and did that excite conscious light, impelling it to increase the speed of change on planet Earth? Is the Quaternary's rapid cycling not Earth having a seizure so much as trembling with excitement?

To explore this, let's begin by looking at those past extinction events.

Logically, the fantastic destruction caused by an extinction event would seem to compel life to start over again, virtually from scratch. But this is not the case. Instead, extinction events generally result in the appearance of better, smarter and more adaptable creatures than were present before they occurred.

The engineer sweeps his blackboard clear for the same reason. He wants to start with a new and better plan. And yet, everything I understand about reality tells me that it's not that simple.

The most famous example of this is what happened after the Permian extinction. For 10 million years after the event, life on Earth struggled with continuing negative conditions on a scale that we can hardly imagine. The land was stripped bare, the atmosphere was foul, the oceans were roiled by fantastic, all but endless storms. Little survived, nothing thrived.

But then, according to a study presented in 2012 in Nature Geoscience, by Zuong-Quiang Chen and Michael Benton, life not only recovered but entirely new species burst forth in millions. It was as if, according to a statement made by Benton on the LiveScience website, "the event had re-set evolution."

Another is the KT Event that destroyed the dinosaurs. When life recovered, mammals, a more advanced and capable genus than the reptiles, became dominant. These creatures, smarter, better designed and more active than the dinosaurs, filled the world with a proliferation of new bodies, minds and events.

Their rise marked the beginning of the next era, the Cenozoic, which is still unfolding. It is divided into the Tertiary, which lasted until 2.8 million years ago and the current period, the Quaternary.

During the Tertiary there was a phenomenal flowering of new species as the mammals raced to replace the dinosaurs.

Then came homo habilis and the upheavals of the Quaternary. There was no definable extinction event then, but when the ice ages began to disrupt the climate, the more exotic and specialized mammalian experiments of the Tertiary began their long period of decline.

This culminated in the extinction event that we are in right now. It started about 13,000 years ago, when an apparent comet strike destroyed most of the large land animals in the northern hemisphere, including almost the entire human population of the American continent.

The upheaval was worldwide, but mankind survived elsewhere, and we immediately filled the niches left by the predators who had not. After we recovered from the shock of the event we proceeded to create larger social organizations than ever before. We see the outcome of this sort of early socialization in the recently discovered Gobekli Tepe monuments, which could not have erected by people who did not possess a complex society. Building began about 2,000 years after the upheaval during a period known in geologic history as the Younger Dryas. What happened was that, about 2,000 years after the glaciers began melting, there was a sudden return to cold conditions. This was followed, 11,500 years ago, by a dramatic temperature spike during which temperatures in Greenland, for example, rose 18 degrees Fahrenheit in just 10 years. Such a change today would lead to worldwide catastrophe, and it did then, too. Thousands of animal species, especially large ones that were dependent on specific ecologies, disappeared.

As a direct result of the fact that this event gave us more room, we have become the dominant species on Earth. I don't think that it is a coincidence that we are also the smartest and among the most adaptable. We are the absolute leading edge of consciousness here, the most self-aware, intelligent and, above all, curious creature the planet has ever produced.

Since the close of the Younger Dryas, Earth has been in an interglacial, and we have benefited from the warm, benign conditions. But we are coming to the end of this period, and this will be a violent event, in part because of the fact that we are pumping so much carbon dioxide into the atmosphere. And don't believe the claims on the internet that CO2 doesn't affect atmospheric heating. These claims are demonstrably false. The fossil record convincingly shows that most past extinction events involved dramatic increases in CO2. Only the one that killed the dinosaurs was definitely caused by an impact.

First, the planet is going to heat up. That's what is happening now. Afterward, sudden cooling will plunge it into another ice age.

Interglacials generally climax with a dramatic temperature spike like this, which is followed by equally sudden cooling. The heating is caused by the release of tremendous amounts of methane "frozen" in hydrates beneath the northern oceans. When the hydrates melt, which occurs at 47 degrees Fahrenheit, trillions of tons of methane gas escape into the atmosphere. Right now, we are just at the point that this process is beginning. Right now methane that has been trapped in permafrost across the arctic is releasing. The methane hydrates beneath the ocean have not yet melted but the current rapid warming of the arctic will cause that to happen.

I ask Anne when it will happen.

"I see towers standing now that will be standing then, so not too far off."

"A hundred years?"

"I see kids in playgrounds. That tells me, within their lifetimes."

"You think in pictures? How does that work?"

"You see the future like that. You can't see things that haven't happened yet, but you can see people whose fates are intertwined with them. We don't see futures, we see fates."

Since human population began exploding in the middle of the 18th Century, our presence has functioned something like a volcano that never stops erupting, adding the intensity of manmade global warming to a natural cycle that has been under way for at least two thousand years. We have, in other words, sped up the climax of the interglacial, and probably by a lot.

We may or may not be able to change this, but we cannot change the underlying cycle. No matter what we do, how long we delay it or do not delay it, the interglacial is destined to end, and with it Earth's ability to support billions of human lives.

It's not our fault any more than we can fix it. What is our fault is that we are neither planning for it nor trying to reduce our own effect on it. The reason we're not acting to save ourselves is very simple. All the debate that goes on around the obvious, demonstrable fact that the planet is warming fast comes down to one thing, which is fear.

Greedy people running companies that pollute fear the loss of their profits. People who feel helpless fear to look at something so horrible that cannot be changed. So we're paralyzed.

"That's part of why we're here. You don't feel fear in our state. We can communicate that by freeing you from the fear of death."

"That would be a start, given that we live in an age of upheaval."

The chaos of alternating interglacials and ice ages are now the natural order of planet Earth, and have fundamentally influenced the evolution of our species, the development of the mind, culture and history. In fact, we owe our existence to the upheaval we are living in. Dealing with the stress of the radical climate cycle we live in is what has given us our minds.

When the most recent glaciation started a hundred and twenty thousand years ago, we were naked, living in small family groups and practicing primitive forms of hunting and gathering. As the climate grew colder, we learned to clothe ourselves. When game became more scarce, we improved our weapon making and hunting skills. Then, around 40,000 years ago something unpredictable happened. The first wave of a nearby supernova seems to have struck the planet. It started with radiation strong enough to kill anything exposed to it, which seared Australia and parts of Asia and Africa for about 24 hours. It continued for weeks, but not a high enough levels to kill.

Not only does radiation kill, however, it also causes a flood of mutations. For example, prior to the supernova we're discussing here, man had only one blood type, type O. During this same period types A and B appeared. The human brain also mutated at about this time.

It was then that Neanderthal man began his decline and Cro-Magnon appeared. He had a new sort of brain: a mutation had occurred that dramatically increased the size of Wernicke's area, which controls comprehension and the semantics of language. This is by far the most important difference between human and ape brains.

That the mutation was sudden is suggested by the abruptness with which Cro-Magnon enters in the fossil record, seemingly almost out of nowhere.

In addition, we now know that another crucial change was taking place, although over a much longer period of time. The NFIX gene, which is what causes the jaw of more primitive forms like the Neanderthal to protrude, was less active in early humans. This meant that, generation after generation, their faces shortened and vocal tracts changed, giving them an increased capacity for speech.

These things meant that Cro-Magnon could evolve complex languages and the correspondingly larger and more viable social groups that are essential to survival in a world of constant change like ours. Was it not for the shortening of the face and the expansion of this brain region, human society, art and culture could never have developed. Language could never have evolved.

It would appear that the supernova created us, or better said, was used as a tool in that process.

"That kind of super-speculation that you do drove me crazy when I was physical and I'm going to repeat now what I used to say then: keep it in question."

Ok, then I think I can say this: Whether or not the radiation flood caused the brain mutation cannot be known, but all across the latter half of the ice age, as Neanderthals slowly disappeared, the vibrant new Cro-Magnons thrived.

Then, 13,000 years ago, the slower moving, solid debris from the supernova swept through our solar system. This caused the fantastic and deadly upheaval on planet Earth that brought the last ice age to its sudden end. In North America, the entire continent was set ablaze, then the ice sheets that covered the region as far south as southern Illinois collapsed, flooding the burning forests and plains.

The result of this is a geologic feature is called the black mat. It is now found at various depths beneath the surface of the soil over much of the United States. This mat consists of ash and other debris combined with the fossils of algae.

What had happened was that the melting ice sheet caused a continental flood that put out the fires. The shallow floodwaters gradually drained away, leaving the debris that was floating on its surface lying on the ground. This dried and hardened into the mat.

All of the large animals that existed in north America except the bears and the bison were destroyed. The Indians who lived here at the time were entirely eliminated, except for those along the coast of the Pacific Northwest.

North America wasn't the only region flooded. All across the planet as the ice melted, flooding occurred. There are more than 50 flood myths worldwide that remember the event. About a thousand years after the catastrophe started, the situation stabilized.

As has happened again and again across the history of our planet, the catastrophe led not to chaos and ruin, but to something much more advanced rising out of the destruction. In this case, it was complex human civilization, agriculture and the beginning of our history and culture.

We have ascended into what is present on Earth today, a vast, complex and immeasurably wealthy human civilization filled with people who are beginning to look at themselves in new ways and, at the extreme edge of evolution, now attempting to forge this new bond between the physical and nonphysical sides of the species, breaking through into a new consciousness that bridges death itself.

However, the civilization we have created is in the process of over-whelming the planet's ability to sustain it. Not only that, as it has become more and more intricate and demanding of resources, it has also become more and more inflexible and vulnerable to sequential collapse, a process that could escalate very quickly into a general cata-strophe.

When I saw this danger some years ago, I wrote the book Super-storm with Art Bell, which led to the movie the Day After Tomorrow. Both were dismissed as being absurdly overdramatic. In 2016, though, prominent climatologist James Hansen and 18 other climate scientists published a paper in Atmospheric Chemistry and Physics entitled "Ice Melt, Sea-Level Rise and Superstorms: evidence from paleoclimate data, climate modeling and modern observations that 2c of global warming could be dangerous."

So the word "superstorm" may have started with a raspberry, but it has entered the language of science, not to say the public conscious-ness after Hurricane Sandy became universally known as Superstorm Sandy.

No matter how it unfolds, we are facing a situation that seems ready to deteriorate so quickly that it is likely to lead to a significant loss of life of all kinds, including human life.

Whether we go entirely extinct in the physical or continue to survive to some extent I cannot say, but we are extremely likely to experience a population decline over the next century or so.

"I can't tell you exact dates, Whitley, but I can tell you that there is survival. The end of a species' life is not death any more than the end of an individual. Extinction is a another aspect of evolution, just like grief is another form of love."

"Say something happens like one of those monster storms. Millions of people are dying. It's hell on Earth. What's that like from your perspective?"

"As I've said, death at your level is birth at ours."

Birth is not pretty and it's not pleasant. It's hard and it's fright-ening and it's dangerous. It is also as much a natural process when it happens to a species as when it happens to an individual.

"Also, just as an individual is born and dies many times, the same is true of a species. When you are no longer subject to physical filters, you can look back over the lives you have lived—the long shadow of your soul—but also to some extent the even longer shadow of the species soul. It lives and dies through incarnations just like individuals do."

I don't know where to go with that. I've never thought of it before. It causes me to realize just how enormous all of this is, and make me wonder if mind unbound is more capable of understanding reality than mind when it has the use of a tool like the brain, or is the opposite the case?

"Life is an organ of soul, Whitley. Living bodies are sensing devices inserted into the river of time, both individuals and whole species. What you think of as yourself is actually a mechanism being controlled by your nonphysical self, which is using it to gain new knowledge. Remember that being is both individual and general. You attend to your own life cycle, but by so doing you also attend to the life cycles of the species, the planet, all the way up to the universe."

Conscious light spreads its rays over the physical world, seeking always deeper, always farther. I can already hear the voices crying in the storm and know, also, that there will be ecstasy riding its winds. The coming forth of mankind will be like that, a great cry and a great terror, but also open eyes here and there, hands reaching across the bridge of love, and death fading into the illusion that it is.

CHAPTER 15

The White Moth

STARTING in the spring of 2016, something began to happen that would end by proving to me that Anne is still a conscious presence. It was brilliantly executed, it was witnessed by others and it could only have emerged out of deep knowledge of the relationship between the two of us.

I found myself in a position to believe—but remember, we are not asking you to do that. What we want you to do is to look at your own life and the life of the world in a new way, to find new sensitivities and with them new questions that belong to your own search and your own exploration of relationship with your loved ones on the other side of the bridge.

In May of 2016 I was at the first public speaking engagement I'd been involved with in years. It was a Saturday, April 9. I was attending a conference in Arkansas. I'd thought that the participants would be indifferent or even hostile to me because I've gone so far past the conventional flying saucer- alien stories, so I had been uneasy about attending. But I found instead people who were interested in the new direction my work had taken, so I was spending a lot of time with them comparing notes and discussing experiences. It was really pretty exciting.

My talk was entitled "A New World If We Can Take It" and was about the fact that a new reality is on offer to us, and what we need to do to take advantage of it—the theme of my and Anne's lives, really.

At the conference, I felt Anne's presence very strongly. I was already communicating with her, but still unsure if it was Anne as a separate, nonphysical entity, or the Anne who is part of my own soul.

I did not yet understand that it was and always will be both. Compared to what it has since become, my understanding of the nonphysical world was primitive then.

When I spoke, it seemed as if she was once more standing beside me. How often in the past we had spoken together like that. We would give our talk and she would read from the Communion Letters, the book that she created from a representative sample of the letters from close encounter witnesses she had read over the years.

Then, on that Saturday afternoon, something unusual and disturbing happened. It had nothing to do with the conference, but rather with the surveillance system in my apartment in Los Angeles. If the cameras observe movement or hear unusual sounds, they send a text to my cell phone. In the years that I've had them, I've received a few such texts, usually indications of unusual sounds, such as a clap of thunder or a nearby dog barking. But this text was different. It warned of movement in the living room.

I at once went to the camera's app on my phone and looked to see what was happening. To my surprise, a large white moth was flitting back and forth in front of the lens. As I watched, it flew back and forth, back and forth. It was about midnight in Arkansas, so 9PM in Los Angeles. The living room was dark. The moth could have been another color, but the camera's infrared light made it appear white.

What was odd about this was that the doors and windows to the apartment were shut up tight and nobody had been in it since I'd left two weeks before. So how had this large moth gotten in?

Over the next twenty-four hours, it came out a number of times, always at night. It still seemed perfectly normal to me. Most moths are nocturnal. It didn't look unusual.

My focus was on finding it and getting it out of my apartment as soon as I returned home. But when I showed the images to some of the conferees, I got something of a surprise. One of them, a psychic, said, "that's no ordinary moth," but he couldn't add more than that. I thought, 'yeah, it's in a place where it shouldn't have been able to get.' I still didn't think that it was anything more than ordinary.

When I returned home, the first thing I did was to search the apartment from top to bottom. No moth. I went through all the closets, pulled out furniture, even looked behind the refrigerator. There was no moth carcass. I left the camera on that night and for the next five nights. No moth.

Maybe, I thought, there was a point of entry that I hadn't seen, and it had left the way it had come. But insects don't behave that way. I should have found it fluttering against a window or dead on a sill.

Over the next year, no matter when the camera was on, the moth did not reappear. I thought nothing more about it.

But then in April of 2017, I took the trip to the campus where I had previously gone while out of my body. During a speech I was giving there, I mentioned Anne—and in that moment, the camera texted my phone.

Literally at the moment I had said the word "Anne," the white moth had passed in front of the living room camera. It briefly alighted on the cabinet where the camera is located, and I could see it well enough to determine that it had the antennae of a silk moth. The *ceanothus* silk moth is found in this region, so there was nothing unusual there.

Over the next few days and nights while I was still traveling, the moth never made another appearance. It had passed in front of the camera just at that one moment.

Given the fact that it was there only when I was talking about Anne, it finally occurred to me that it might have something to do with her. When I returned home, I once again made a search for remains. This time, I was extremely careful and methodical, going through closets, looking behind furniture, under the edges of rugs, behind appliances— anywhere it might have fallen.

Once again when I arrived home the apartment had been shut up tight, and once again nothing was found, except for the dried carcass of a different and much smaller species of moth that had been dead for a long time.

I stood in the middle of the apartment. I was at a loss. Finally I asked her, "Do you have anything to do with this?"

I didn't hear a reply—I was only just learning how to detect the flavor of her thoughts and could not 'channel' her. But there came into my mind, and quite forcefully, a memory of my short story "The White Moths."

Anne had loved it. She thought it the best of my short stories.

Now I reflected that the only time in a year that the white moth had appeared was a moment that I had mentioned her name. In a year!

I heard her laughter—that gut-deep, solid laugh of hers that I had so enjoyed when she was alive. Then she said, "I can talk to you."

I was shocked. That voice had not been part of me, it had come as if somebody else was speaking in my mind, somebody besides me.

That night we talked and talked like we were two excited kids again, just discovering each other. I wanted to tell her of my daily life as it has been since she passed, but that didn't interest her. She was interested only in my inner life, with special emphasis on learning to love myself objectively.

I found out that night that my wife is still a marvelous teacher, ready with penetrating questions but very careful with advice. She is not a "guide." She seeks to help one guide oneself.

That night and the next day and night passed in illuminating dialogue. I finally got used to it. I want to say that I could now tell for certain that it was her, and in my own mind that is true, but she would never let me settle into belief. Just like a moth, her mind fluttered here and there, never resting, always seeking toward the light and urging me along with her.

Still, though, there was that edge of doubt. Could this really be true? Really?

The next weekend I was with my son, who lives a hundred miles away. Since I'd gotten back from my trip to the campus, I had left the camera on day and night. The moth had not appeared either on camera or visually.

Anne had a lovely relationship with her son. As a little one, as a teen, as a young man, she was very, very good at giving him the kind of room and the clear limits that a kid needs. Her mothering was gentle, always, her advice for him full of wisdom.

In all the years of his growing up, she not only never punished him, she never so much as raised her voice to him. She didn't act toward him as if he was somehow less a person because he was a child. She respected his rights and expanded them as he matured. She disciplined him by being disappointed when he did not meet those expectations. Then she would guide him so gently back in the right direction.

Their love was deep and beautiful, a work of art between mother and son, dancing with humor and full of the ordinary excitement that attaches to a child's discovery of the world.

By this time, May of 2017, when I would go to visit him and his kids, I would feel very strongly that she was with me.

Mom always came, too.

On this afternoon, also a Saturday, I was sitting with him and telling him of what had happened during my speech of a week before, and of my suspicion that Anne was somehow behind the appearances of the moth.

I explained to him that "the White Moths," is a meditation on the time of dying and what it means to really live life, and also what it means to live in life's illusions, and how much mom liked it.

I said, "Anyway, I'm thinking that maybe it all has something to do with mother."

In that instant, the camera texted me. It had detected movement.

I turned on the app. At the exact moment that I had said "maybe it all has something to do with mother," the white moth had passed in front of the camera.

When we saw the image of the little creature fluttering past, it was like looking into the depths of an unknown truth.

It did not appear again, not on that day and not for weeks. Just that once, just in front of the camera, then gone. The camera has a wide-angle lens that covers the whole living room. The moth flew past that lens approximately six inches from it and disappeared.

I felt my beloved Anne fill my heart. Then tears came. I didn't want to upset my son, so I fell silent, trying to control myself.

He sat a long time in silence also. Then said softly, gently,

"Mom, I love you."

The reality was hard for me to deny. No, impossible. For there is much more to the white moth than even these appearances.

So here I was at the end of a question. I knew, now: Anne is still here. She is still conscious and she is involved with her family.

"And with lots of people," she adds as I write. "I get around."

"Do you talk to people?"

"That's not how it works. You talk in them, not to them. Sometimes you influence them, mostly you don't. The ego is like a radio turned up too loud. You have to tune it down or you can't hear us."

Like everything that comes from her, these few words are filled with teaching. Not guidance or future-telling, but solid, practical teaching about how this new kind of relationship looks from her side and how it can be made to work.

The use of the white moth as a symbol is very canny and very smart. Somehow, she could influence the creature. Maybe she even conjured it. To this day, I've never found a single sign of a moth like that anywhere in the apartment.

"The White Moths" is a contemplation of death in which the white moths symbolize the spirits of the dead and life is seen as a journey in illusion.

Anne says at this moment, "You'd be amazed at how true that is. The first thing that happens when you look back on your life isn't that dour contemplation they talk about—the life review. You realize that you took it too seriously. It's a game. That's life. Looking back on that serious, ambitious, frustrated little creature that you were is amazing and puzzling. That was me, that little thing with its tiny problems? Going into the physical causes you to forget the great scale of your own being. You touch that in "the White Moths" and that's why I love it. Consider that white moth of mine my philosophical statement about the true nature of physical experience."

There is also a mention of white moths in "Song of the Wandering Aengus:"

"...when white moths were on the wing, And moth-like stars were flickering out, I dropped the berry in a stream And caught a little silver trout."

Just as my white moth initiated my search, his white moths began his.

Most recently, when I was staying with friends in Texas, the white moth would fly across the camera's field of view just once every time I started to meditate. It was as if to say, 'You're away from home but I'm still with you.'

In choosing the white moth as the "word" she used to express herself into physical life, she opened up a richness of meaning that derives not only from my own creative urge and from her defining statement about the search that will occupy the rest of my life, but also from a treasury of symbolic meaning that crosses the cultures of the world.

In ancient Greece, the word psyche was used both for soul and for moth. But it goes much deeper, in that Psyche was also thought of as anima mundi, the animating spirit of the world. After hearing my story, philosopher and friend Dr. Patricia Turrisi wrote me, "Psyche signifies at the same time soul and butterfly. The myth was interpreted by playing on this double sense. It became the story of the soul touched by divine love, but which, by reason of the mistakes made, must undergo some tribulations before having access to happy immortality. The night butterfly (the moth) attracted by the flame, like the soul attracted by heavenly truths, burns in the flame, reflection of the trials that must be endured to eliminate the fleshy sink- stones before knowing the joys of the beyond."

It is those joys to which Anne has been preparing to ascend. Now, judging from a contact with her that has just unfolded, she is ready to make her onward journey.

I have long since passed beyond the notion that all dreams are "just dreams" and have learned to respect the power of a disciplined imagination. As we have gone soul blind, we have also lost the knowledge that, while dreams may be dreams, they may also be journeys into other worlds, most particularly the land where our dead dwell.

As I write these words I am just back from such a journey.

It started with a surprise meeting with a glowing woman, very beautiful, and her brother. I have not met them in physical life, but I learned their names and saw their faces. They introduced themselves carefully, but when I asked for a last name, they only smiled. I knew why: if I had that piece of information, our fates would be interrupted, and our fates are to meet, if we do, by chance.

It was a poignant, lovely moment when she smiled at me and I saw in that smile hope and pride, the pride of beauty, not only of the body but also of the soul. I could feel her seeking toward me.

I said, "I'm already married."

They showed me their lives. They were lovely people, living somewhere that seemed to me to be typically American, prosperous, comfortable and settled. As I went with them, seeing their friends, the children and parents in their lives, I experienced at once the pleasure of their peace and an aching sense of separation from Anne.

I wear both of our wedding rings to symbolize that we are now sharing the one body. I expect that to last for the rest of my life, and on my death to unite with Anne forever.

But if I meet these people, as I understand it, I am going to find a new destiny. I am going to start a new physical life in their family. The woman will fall in love with me and I with her. I will continue on into a new marriage.

As was my meeting with Anne, it's primarily a matter of the ambiguous nature of reality which is so crucial to the surprise that makes life worth living, that we call chance.

I could imagine myself falling in love with this woman. I could imagine it, but I don't want to. The idea brings me a homesickness more acute than any such emotion I felt during childhood, lying in my bunk on summer camp nights, watching the moon slide past the window and longing to be in my own bed.

Then I found myself, in the dream, with Anne. There have not been very many such direct meetings. I was about to laugh with her about "some woman" trying to seduce me when I noticed a new sense about her. I said, "You seem more free."

She replied, "Yes. I'm going on now. This was a beautiful marriage and I will always love you, but we're all part of nature and the marriage is ending."

This simply shattered me—right in the middle of the "dream."

The woman came, hesitant, wanting to comfort me and draw me into the gentle possession of a new love.

I thought no, no, it can't be true. And as I write, my eyes are filling with the same tears that filled them when we walked that path in the land of the soul. I said, "I don't want it to end."

But then I realized a truth, that marriage is about bodies and the heat of bodies, life and children. You do not stay married across the bridge. You build a new kind of companionship, dear and loyal but not exclusive like physical marriage.

I felt Anne touch me on my arm. It was electrifying and terribly sweet, poignant beyond expression. She said, "Don't be afraid, honey, we'll always be together."

"Don't leave me!"

But just as she had on the night she died, she went on, walking easily toward a new world and a new life that I cannot imagine.

I must remain here to do my work in our family and in the physical world of which I am still a part. And if I should ever meet that lovely woman, I will find another courtship and a new life path.

Anne said, "Keep looking always, never forget your search. You gave me everything you have to give, Whitley, and here I am in this immortal state."

"You gave me everything, too."

"I'm still a teacher." I could feel a closeness between us then, a new aspect of life across the bridge. These teachers we so absurdly call "the dead" teach from within our own minds and souls, standing ready to take us deeper than it has ever before been possible to go, into lands and knowledge yet distant, but which are meant for us to know. We will learn to be as these beings we call aliens are, living in the physical and nonphysical states both at the same time, as a whole species.

Such happiness was flowing out of her as we walked that I laughed through my tears, a delight of anguish.

But then—then—she began to walk on ahead. I couldn't keep up. I tried and tried but she rose from the land of the dream just as she had on the night she died, ascending farther and farther.

I woke up in an ocean of tears.

It was three in the morning, the hour of meditation. Still in tears, I rose from my bed and went to the chair where I meditate, did the sensing exercise and went deep.

New love came flowing into me, a fine, careful love that is aimed squarely at the strengthening of my soul. It was no longer the love of a wife, though, but that of a dear teacher and friend, the best I could ever know.

"Will you leave me now?"

She shook her hips provocatively. It sure didn't look like somebody who was leaving me, not even physically. But that's not true, as I have come to understand. The freedom we both need is for me to accept that I am physical and have physical needs that I cannot simply long for her to fulfill. I may or may not fulfill them, but I cannot continue to ask her to be my marriage partner. When the physical body ends, so does the physical marriage.

On the other hand, the deeper one between souls needs never end.

But it is not exclusive, not like physical marriage. Anne's soul belongs to the world in different way now.

We have found a new kind of relationship together, the teacher learning, as all good teachers do, along with the student. For she, also, has a journey ahead of her, to fulfill her essential destiny, helping in the great work of drawing souls— many souls—through the alembic of life and into joy.

I know she will do her work very well. She is so good at it. But my girl will always be my girl, slipping now ahead of me along the path. I want so badly to keep up, but I belong still to the physical and must stay here like a old lump. My soul can soar, but never high enough. And yet, even though I see her far away, I feel her with such intimacy, a ghostly presence soaring within me, that it makes me howl out my longing.

I take in my heart now the last lines of Aengus, the defining song of my search:

> "Though I am old with wandering
> Through hollow lands and hilly lands,
> I will find out where she has gone,
> And kiss her lips and take her hands;
> And walk among long dappled grass,
> And pluck till time and times are done,
> The silver apples of the moon,
> The golden apples of the sun."

Fare you well, dear soul, more to me than I am to myself. I will follow along as best I can in the path you are laying. I will find you in my memory and the turnings of my mind and in your whispering, laughing voice, so rich with wisdom and so very kind.

As you said so often and so well, great love never ends.

At this moment, seemingly by chance as I write the last words of this book, I see that it is August 11, 2017. It is 7:25PM, exactly two years to the minute since you rose through my arms and began your journey.

I belong still to Earth and you now to heaven, but I know that you will always be there when I call to you across the bridge, for the love that we share will carry my voice into that smiling country, the mysterious land of light where you dwell.

The End

Anne and Whitley Strieber

Appendix 1

The Love that Led Me Home by Anne Strieber

I would like to tell you a story that seems to me to have helped almost everybody I have told it to, and has certainly helped me.

I have gone on a long and dangerous journey into an unknown world. I don't remember much about it, except one thing that is extremely clear: I remember a point at which I was given a choice. There was a natural desire to live and survive, and I was looking for ways to do it. But I think that if I hadn't found a guide, I wouldn't have made it.

The guide turned out to be my beloved cat Coe. I remember weeping into his fur when I finally had to put him to sleep after a long bout with cancer. Coe was always the family clown. He had no instincts. He didn't fall on his feet. He was very smart, and quite capable of lying.

Once there was a terrific crash in the living room, and Coe came strolling into the family room elaborately yawning as if he'd just waked up. The catastrophe in the living room, we were supposed to believe, couldn't have had anything to do with a peacefully sleeping cat.

I was very surprised to encounter Coe. I didn't really see him, but more sensed his presence. I knew that I was at the juncture between life and death. It was a busy place, and I wasn't sure Coe would even wait for me.

There seemed to be very little time. At that point, in the physical world, I began trying to call my son on the cellphone, or so I thought. I later discovered that he was at my bedside. It was as if I was living in two worlds at once. I wanted to tell him that Coe was here, because I thought he'd be very excited. They were close, close friends, those two.

I'd always expected to see my dead mother. She passed away when I was only seven, so I don't remember her much at all. I'd been waiting for this moment all my life, because I want to see her and remember her. I've always thought that I would see her again after death, and remember her then. And yet, she wasn't at the center of my love. Her death was just so long ago, and I was so little when it happened.

I certainly had a lot of love with Coe and I was so glad to see him, but right now he was very matter of fact.

It was as if he was saying, "C'mon, there's no time to waste." I was left with the impression that animals know the secret of life and death far better than we do.

I heard him say inside my head, "These STUPID humans--Don't even know how to find the World of the Dead on their own!" He took me to a place that looked like a subway or Greyhound bus station, an underground waiting room lit with those weird yellowish lights you see in such places. The place was busy: I had the impression of lots of people around, and that they were clutching bulging shopping bags and suitcases, maybe the memories they wanted to bring with them from life.

And I somehow knew that they weren't going to be able to go on (to catch that subway or bus) until they were willing to put their packages DOWN.

To Coe, it was nothing special at all. It wasn't as if he thought of himself as a spirit guide or anything. It was much more casual and matter-of-fact than that. He was ready to take me down a certain path if I wanted to go, and there was love, but it wasn't filled with elaborate new emotions.

He never functioned well as a cat, mousing and that sort of thing. But he was the world's best cuddler, little boy playmate, and friend of the heart and soul. And now he was here, ready to take me for a little stroll into the beyond.

After he died, he showed up in our apartment a few days later. Whitley, who sees such things, saw him and saw that he was lost. He took him and pointed him toward the other world, that now seems to me as much a part of ordinary life as it is for Whitley. Now he was back, ready to help me take the same journey.

I think that the reason for this happening is that there has been an investment of real love. I put love into Coe, and he loved me, and that love now has an independent life. Maybe it wasn't even Coe there, really. Maybe he found the path long ago, and is far down it now. But the love was left behind, waiting for me until I needed it.

It took a journey beyond the edge of life and the help of a little animal to bring me to a place of new understanding, that all that really survives of us is the love we have made in the world. It's a simple truth that will stay with me forever, even when I pass again across the threshold, this time never to return. Especially then.

Appendix 2

The White Moths by Whitley Strieber

What to do? There was the coffee cup needing to be washed, and the bed could do with a smoothing. There were those buggy roses. And a letter to Janie, yes, there was that to do.

She watched the sunlight instead, creeping about in the lawn. How long had she known this light in this lawn? Nineteen thirty-one to nineteen eighty-seven. How on earth long was that? Thirty one, forty one...over fifty years.

Damned long, you old coot. Funny. You have gotten old. Become old, it sounds better. And what of your phoebes, there in their nest in the old grape arbor? You have been watching that pair of phoebes-- well, always.

She realized with a bit of a dry chill that her little friends had probably gone through dozens of generations in that ruin of an arbor. She had not made pets of a pair of birds, not over fifty years. She had made pets of a whole line of birds, stretching back into the dark past.

Now why hadn't she realized that before? She had been feeding them for over half a century, all through Bob's life, from when he was a young husband bounding up those stone steps until he was a thing of rattling papyrus with his pain and his awful grasping.

Here she was alone in this comfortable old house, well, banging around a little, really, but content with her diet of mystery stories and waiting for the evening news.

She watched the hopeless folly of Presidents, one after the other failing in some manner, and thought it odd that nobody seemed to notice that every one of them since Johnson had come a-cropper. The whole institution had failed. Another symptom of dying.

A flock of geese appeared in the northern sky, nothing but a brush of dots but she knew what they were, oh yes, the geese of October again. She ran her finger along the window sill, wondering at the white dust. Natalie would be disturbed; she kept this place so carefully, the blessed soul.

There was that letter to write. She stood up and moved through the great shadows to her old roll-top, the desk where Bob had spent so many hours doing his evening work. There were burns from his cigars, and still in the secret drawer there was that little flask of cognac, untouched since last she refilled it for him so many years ago.

She took paper and pen--her own pretty paper with the blue crest--and laid the nib against the white sheet.

"My Dear Janie," she wrote, "I am so afraid."

She stopped. Now what trick of hand or mind was this? She had not intended to write those words. No, certainly not. Afraid? Never. She was not afraid. Death would come soon, of course, but one went on.

She regarded the words she had written. What nonsense. She hadn't meant to write that. Still, there had been the softest,

gentlest dream, had there not, of those--well--perhaps...

A white moth fluttered suddenly up from some cranny in the desk, a moth so swift and pale. She brushed it away. It came again, swarming at her face. She batted at it. Yet again it appeared, fluttering, its legs scrabbling at her cheeks, her eyes, as if it had mistaken her face for a route of escape. She pushed the chair back, batted with both hands, then stood up.

She had thought to go down to the kitchen for the fly swatter--surely it would work against a moth--but the thing appeared to be gone.

Moths were not a good sign. She thought of what they could do to her furs, the lynx, the minks, the white wolf she had worn so many years ago in Paris...the Opera Steps...

She grasped air, thinking of the balustrade, of touching it lightly as she descended into the bright interval throng. And had not Willy D'Orsay glanced up at her and smiled his benign, perfectly naughty smile?

UNTITLED

How odd to remember him, an acquaintance of half an hour...She had danced with him at the Club--which damned club--or was that aboard the Mary? Danced. "Talking band," he'd said. And she'd said, "yes!"

She must not let the moths get at her coats, not at her beautiful white wolf, the furs bought from that poor Russian man, the one who jumped from the hotel window and had the misfortune to live. But the Nazis finished him, as they did all of the cripples of Paris.

An American in Paris. She saw herself reflected in the window as she crabbed about hunting the moth. But there were her coats to think about, her gowns, her frocks, the smooth cloths for the skin of girlhood.

And what wisdom have you gained, you who teeter here, ghastly old creature smelling of drought and Listerine? What wisdom?

She knew about politics. She had always voted. Landon slide. She remembered that, but he had not won. No, it was FDR again, that raging cripple, as angry in his way as the Russian with the white wolf furs, spreading them across the dining table in the Crillon suite, the perfect, white furs of six wolves, how extraordinary and she had been so clever with him. "Well, they are good, but I am not paying retail."

"No, madame, of course not," and he a duke once before the destruction of the Empire. Madame, and he a duke once. She had taken the furs for nothing--nothing--a few dollars, and now that white moth--

She moved quickly, maneuvering her leaden body about the room, wondering if the moth had come in the window, or somehow popped into life inside Bobby's old desk, that wretched old thing full of cigar smell and tin boxes with keys to here and there, abandoned sheds and hunting cabins up in the hills and all of his intricate, leathery things, his boxes of moldering papers, his safe full of damned stamps.

Oh, he lay so still that morning.

The white moth flew round and round her head and she saw it clearly, a pale thing, so soft...with tiny eyes as red as they could be. Tiny, red eyes, alien, cold and strange, eyes that brought the stars to mind.

Billy had enjoyed peering at the stars with his telescope. He'd get up at two in the morning and hunt with his dogs until dawn, then come back for eggs and bacon and coffee. Then off he'd go to the office or come in here and work until noon, then lunch and a heavy nap and more work until four, then drinks.

Drinks...the flower garden in the summer, the white chairs, her cool dresses, the girls in their summer things, and Woodrow serving the bourbon and water and the chunky ice when it came delivered then, and those wonderful little salted things that Jenny made--what were those things? And politics were discussed. She had taken to reading the papers, the New York Tribune, then it became the Herald-Tribune, so that she could agree with him intelligently.

Landon slide. Win with Willkie. FDR. Truman blowing up all of those sinister Japanese. She'd never made it to Japan after all. She'd meant to go. Maybe next year. There was no longer a boat, you had to fly and in airplanes they treated you like a dog, those awful supercilious girls in their little blue suits with their trays of dubious food, and the droning and the shaking. The Weedens had gone down.

She sat, suddenly, in a dark gothic bishop's chair. "It is not enough," she said in a calm, clear voice, "to be afraid."

She was old and ugly and her eyes were like two piercing blades of obsidian. Her children disliked her and her mere presence terrified the grandchildren.

One ends up wearing one's sins on the face. The easy laughter, the indiscreet tone, the gobbled life--it all floats to the face like scum to the surface of a pool. Had she known when she was thirty what she knew now of herself she would have followed that miserable Russian right out the hotel window.

Now she took long oil baths, telling the cosmetician at Fallow's that she wanted the oils for her daughter, for Janie, or for her grand-daughter Mary. Her fingers were long and smooth again in the bathroom light, her arms round and gleaming, and the oil would slip along her skin. She would be left smelling of gardenia or chamomile or hyacinth. Hadn't somebody called her his hyacinth girl?

She wanted too much, she knew that, but her life had made her that way. It had been so perfect and yet so hard, the deaths in war, the men who were young and made one breathless who died in ditches or screaming in those horrible little airplanes. Somebody had sent back a picture of Timmy Trogget from France, that horrible picture of him so burned. The picture had come anonymously and why, didn't they know that she was a flower and innocent and not to be worried by the ghastly glamour of the front?

Tommy had a ukulele of course--they all had them, that group of boys before the war. He also had a lovely sporting carriage--what was that called--and they would go trotting through the park. His driver was named Waldo. Waldo Salt.

The white moth circled her head and she knew that it was a terrible thing. She began to move out of the room. But the light was long and golden in the gnarled garden, late sun drawing memories from the ruins, and didn't she get already a whiff of some night-blooming flower? No, of course not, November, well. She could well imagine the wolf coat becoming a repository for moth eggs. Who would have known, that beloved masterpiece with her perfume still clinging to it at four o'clock in the morning.

She would be eating scrambled eggs and bacon and drinking coffee with Gladys and Amy and Bob and the Booth brothers, what laughter then and oh yes, that was after the war and everybody had forgotten that poor Trogget boy. Jimmy Andrus had come back from the Hat in the Ring Squadron and not a mark, so perhaps Trogget with his tongue looking like a burst sausage had simply been too slow. He was always too analytical, poor boy.

She wondered if the young and beautiful went on in shadowy consort when they died. Did Trogget come home upon a ship of air and live out the rest of his intended life as if it was real.

Carefully, she placed a chair in the center of the room and climbed it, intending to slap the white moth between her two hands. It fluttered gaily, darting and flashing around the yellow chandelier. She drew her hands apart and slapped them together just as it flew past. The chair rocked, she tottered, regained herself and made another slap at the creature. It was so tiny, so unequal to the battle, and yet it fluttered still, a saucy little flag of a thing. She was furious at it.

Sweeping her hand through the air she tried to scoop it up, but the white moth eluded her again. It flew so fast that it seemed to multiply, ten white moths, a thousand, fluttering in the yellow light of the chandelier. She waved her arms.

She was already falling when she noticed that the chair was no longer beneath her. She hit with a dry crunch and an awful giving-way deep in her back. The parquet floor felt like concrete, despite the fact that a lovely old Bokhara from grandmother's house was spread across it. She heard a voice utter a cry and knew that it was her own.

Then she became aware of a complex sort of pain. She was surprised at how it clarified everything; she had not known much pain in her life.

There had been that time with Saucy Dill, riding in that funny little car of hers--the Dills were ruined right after the crash--when she had dangled her hand against some sort of pipe that extended along the running board. Oh, yes, that was a burn and that had hurt.

This hurt more fundamentally and the treatment would be more elaborate than a cold poultice and a tumbler of bootleg gin. Oh, jazz, what happened to that music, to the days and nights of jazz? The jeweled cascade of years, the dances, the boys, the girls in their frocks...

How does it end, this mystery? Does agony strip away all the romance? That German boy, Knutt VonHauer had sent her his photograph in forty-something--or wasn't it earlier, had to be before the war--standing in the hatch of his tank with his arm raised high and Ruthie had whispered that he looked penile like that. Penile. After the war he became a railway worker. Somebody, Willy or somebody like that, had encountered him on the wagons-lits to Hamburg, turning down the beds!

Later he was living with that philosopher in the Languedoc, wasn't he. Knutt was a man of forty with white, white hair. That Hitler, honestly.

She realized that she would have to get up or rest forever among the hungry white moths. What had been the use of it all, and why had it ended so quickly? A life, just like that. It had seemed fun, but what did that mean? There seemed to be a darkness entering the air, the ceiling of the room rising and parting like two uncupping hands and she was there on a little black cabaret stage in a sinister and compromising pose. What awful things she had done. She had to face that. Gossip, rumors, the ruin of souls. She had brought the whole world tumbling down around her, sweeping her arms about with destructive abandon, destroying the boys of the wars like white moths themselves oh, they were so lovely in their uniforms, the wastes of uniforms marching across the fields like mad, besotted animals singing and then in the awful, private squalor of the front lines.

She wondered if a bullet in the back felt like this. Had she not sent Jimmy or somebody candied fruit at the front and had he not written back that fruit at the front was only eaten by fruits? His captain had written to that awful woman--what was her name, the one with the persistent warts on her fingers--that he had died from lighting a cigarette at the wrong moment.

Died, died, did it matter? She looked up toward the chandelier and thought perhaps that it did not matter. There, in the shadows where the ceiling had been, was there not some clarity, something startling up there among all those swarming masses of moths?

The heat in the house had failed. Wasn't this December? Or was it already January? When was this, what hour, what day, what year? How long had she been like this, adrift in the years? She struggled against the crunching pale rug, trying to rise to have some tea and perhaps some really nice sandwiches, something spicy and nice. Fortnum's and those faintly sinful teas, the perfect ladies, the girls in their--who was that, who had done something outrageous in Fortnum's, that heavy girl from Montclair who had gone to London in search of a Lord but had married a hatter instead? Mad Hatter Harry, but he had worked out very well in Montclair with his high English manners, selling automobiles.

She wanted rather a lot to get back on her feet. But there was a

UNTITLED

mystery: she was trapped in this flying room, its rococo weight borne upon the wings of moths.

Was death as banal as this, nothing more than a brief struggle on a rug? She might soil herself, she thought. No, not that, it was such an abnegation; she did not want to be found like that by the servants, that wicked little maid Natalie with her implacable, penetrating eyes. What did she know? Why had she come here? What awful thing was her soul here to avenge?

It was terrifying to think that one might have wronged somebody in another life, only to find oneself at their mercy later. She suspected that Natalie would take a chair, light a cigarette and simply watch her die.

Her whole life had been an ocean of death. You young people, you don't know anything. History was poison in my time. I lost so many friends, the grandeur of three generations, Princes in their white uniforms jammed into darkened trains, leaders of men and artists-- and what about that wonderful satirist Guttman--after the war nobody mentioned him--and the French milord, that lovely man with his grace and his extraordinary knowledge of horses, that man-- nobody mentioned him.

Couldn't there be some sort of service for the century, perhaps up at Norman Vincent Peale's church, some sort of hopeful little thing?

Bob. Come here. Help me.

A really terrible pain, as red as the moth's silly eyes, came up from her deeps. She had laid on the wide bed and open wide herself and Bob in the darkness with his dry, soft hands and his shirt still on, and had there not been then a flowering tree? A flowering tree...was it a tulip tree?

No. That was in Louisiana, in Grande Coteau in that house by the river when the mist of night came and the river boats passed in the moonlight, and it was so wonderfully stifling and their skin was as slick as ice, hot ice. She had spread herself wide and thrown back her arms and known the delicious smoke of the night down there where never had there been light, and he had lit the gas lamp in the wall, the

194

sputtering yellow flame and she had danced on the bed to his opalescent eyes.

Gleaming things, slick things, her hands moved along the concrete rug, seeking him. She would hold him by the hour, hold and hold until she slept and would awaken still holding. You--I thought--passive--he would say--passive--his whole mind lurking in the syllables. Oh, yes, Bob was predatory. You saw the sores occasionally that marked his secret conquests, and you knew of the relations between him and the New Orleans whores.

She had been glad to leave the south, to come back to these perfect Connecticut hills, to the apartment in the city and the black Packard and the immense power of his parent's wealth. Oil, they would say, Bob found oil and brought us all back to life. She thought of them, those rich, lying in quiet living caskets after the crash while Bob toiled in the alligator swamps in his boots and jodhpurs, directing men to drill here and drill there. And that guttering Ford car they had then, guttering and rattling and behind your back you could feel the springs...

Men and women do not die, they are harvested. They are harvested by the shadows, who live in the enigma. Unlike cattle, men and women if allowed might understand their predicament. What does it matter to the hog who is being scratched behind the ears by a kindly farmer that he will be next month's rasher? What warped, confused logic must append to his comprehension of the meaning of the love and sudden slaughter? How can it make sense to him, all the warm slops and then the axe?

The moths were terrible now, swirling in the light, settling on her shoulders, on her arm, in her hair, crawling coldly down her neck. She could not scream, dared not open her mouth, could not weep, had no tears left. Only Bob, she wanted Bob to come and be young with her again.

I really loved you all those years. I loved you, you damn man with your whores and your conquests and the smells of cigars and leather and the high grouse hanging by the kitchen door. You, you--what did the whores offer that I could not offer? I gave you me and you went and got crusty sores from crusty whores. I was a lily, o man.

I thought that I was nice. Perhaps I was a little plain of face, yes, and maybe it was--position, appropriateness, that made you marry me--and you remained so calm that night in Grand Coteau when I was transported to such an extreme of desire. After your perfectly creditable love, we spoke in the moony dark of Wendell Willkie and oh I was so sad.

The forties...the fifties...the sixties...we thought the years were bright; how little we knew of the cave we were entering. The cave and the rising lazy smoke of those days, perfect ghostly trails into the air-- all the air, all over the world.

I am afraid. What is that shadow?

The two policemen walked together through the flying snow, passing under a radiant street light, then going deeper into the night.

"Look at that pile of snow over there," said the older man. The rookie stared at it. "What should I be seeing?"

"It's a body, son."

"Christ. I didn't know the street people got this far uptown."

"Them bag ladies is everywhere. This one, she's gone and froze to death in the snow."

Made in the USA
Las Vegas, NV
26 October 2021